Unpolished Gem

Alice Pung

Portobello
BOOKS

First published by Portobello Books Ltd 2008
This paperback edition published 2009

Portobello Books Ltd
Twelve Addison Avenue
Holland Park
London W11 4QR, UK

First published in Australia by Black Inc., an imprint of Schwartz
Publishing in 2006.

A CIP catalogue record is available from the British Library

9 8 7 6 5 4 3 2 1

ISBN 978 1 84627 144 1

www.portobellobooks.com

Designed by Thomas Deverall

Offset by Avon DataSet Ltd, Bidford on Avon, Warwickshire

Printed in the UK by CPI Bookmarque, Croydon, CR0 4TD

UNPOLISHED GEM

From the international reviews of *Unpolished Gem*:

'Pung presents the everyday reality of prejudice and assimilation that many migrants face adapting to western culture. Her narrative flits between sobering truths and laugh out loud humour.' ***Big Issue***

'There is something striking on every page.' Helen Garner

'For a book so preoccupied with fraught emotions – both exposed and hidden, and including Pung's own crises – *Unpolished Gem* possesses the steadiest of heartbeats. Somehow Pung achieves a tone both lush and raw, revealing a depth of observation that is intricate yet accessible, unyielding yet generous. She unleashes sardonic humour that avoids condescension. Most of all, she encapsulates and energises whole scenes with a single sentence. This is virtuoso storytelling.' ***The Australian***

'A memoir so vivid that images from it linger behind your eyelids. The stories are full of pain – she starts to go mad in ways that recall the young Vera Brittain in *Testament of Youth* – but there is a rich vein of comedy running through it.' *The Age*

'*Unpolished Gem* is a warm, humorous, but at times heartbreaking story of the migrants' world... The story gives an honest and vibrant account of one family's experiences, with beautiful anecdotes and reflective history. *Unpolished Gem* is a book for today, describing the journey that so many have taken' *Aesthetica magazine*

'Intelligent and touching' *The Herald Sun*

'*Unpolished Gem* takes up where books such as Jung Chang's *Wild Swans* leave off. A delightful read and a funny, touching debut from a writer we're sure to hear more from.' *Brisbane Courier Mail*

'Pung's memoir of her parents' and grandmother's flight from China and Cambodia in the 1970s, and of her childhood in suburban Melbourne, is the spiritual descendant not so much of Jung Chang's *Wild Swans* as of Sylvia Plath's *The Bell Jar*. Pung displays the latter's gift for deliciously wry humour and passionate, pungent prose... like Plath, she manoeuvres mesmerically between the hilarious and the heartbreaking. Her memoir is funny, engrossing and astonishingly wise.' *Sunday Times*

To my family, for this story.
And to Rebecca, who loved to read.

PROLOGUE

This story does not begin on a boat.

We begin our story in a suburb of Melbourne, Australia, in a market swarming with fat pigs and thin people. The fat pigs are hanging from hooks, waiting to be hacked into segments, and the thin people are waiting to buy these segments wrapped in newspaper over a glass counter. When they haggle over the price of trotters, there is much hand-gesticulating and furrowing of brow because the parties do not spick da Ingish velly good. "Like a chicken trying to talk to a duck," my mother calls these conversations. But she is not here today to quack over quality pigs' paws because she is lying in a white hospital room waiting for me to arrive.

So it's just my father, standing smack-bang in the middle of this market, and his shoes are getting wet because of the blood diluted in the water that comes from the huge hoses used to wash away the mess at the end of the day. He looks down at the grates and thinks about pig's blood jelly and whether he'll ever buy it again. He likes the taste, but Ah Ung told him that he worked in the abattoir when he first came here and the carcasses were hung from hooks with buckets beneath to collect the pigs' blood. Because they were not washed properly, they would sometimes leak with piss and other filthy drips. My father does not think back to Phnom Penh, where he would be eating brains in broth made by street vendors stationed across the road from the homeless leper coughing out half a lung in the doorway of some derelict shopfront, but looks up and points at the pink and red appendages behind the glass. With his other hand, he holds up two fingers.

This is the suburb where words like *and*, *at* and *of* are redundant, where full sentences are not necessary. "Two kilo dis. Give me seven dat." If you were to ask politely, "Would you please be so kind as to give me a half-kilo of the Lady Fingers?" the shop-owner might not understand you. "You wanna dis one? Dis banana? How many you want hah?" To communicate, my father realises, does not merely mean the strumming and humming of vocal cords, but much movement of hands and contortion of face. The loudest pokers always win, and the loudest pokers are usually women. My father's moment is lost when a middle-aged woman with Maggi-noodle curls points at the man behind the counter with a flailing forefinger and almost jabs out an eye as she accuses the other Non-English-Speaking Person of selling her furry trotters. "Why yu gib me dis one? Dis one no good! Hairy here, here and dere! Hairy everywhere! Dat nother one over dere better. Who you save da nother one for hah?" Bang on the counter goes the bag of bloodied body parts, and my father knows that now is the time to scoot away to the stall opposite if he wants hairless ham.

This suburb, Footscray, has possibly the loudest and grottiest market in the Western world, although that term doesn't mean much when you're surrounded by brown faces. Footscray Market is the only market where you can peel and eat a whole mandarin before deciding whether to buy a kilo; where you can poke and prod holes in a mango to check its sweetness. My father does not even bat an eye at the kid who is covering her face with one hand, holding out a wet peeled lychee with the other, and wailing "Aaarghhh! My eyeball!" to her little brother. He watches as the baby in the pram starts howling and the mother pulls off some grapes from a stand to shut him up while she goes on with her poking and prodding and justified pilfering. Parsimonious women aren't going to spend four dollars on sour strawberries simply because they were too stupid to taste-test them first. "Cause you more trouble coming back the second time!" declares my mother. "Ayyah, no good to be tormented by four dollars! Try and avoid it if you can." But there is no way to taste-test these trotters, my father thinks as he looks through the clear plastic bag, so he has to take the word of the shouting woman in the opposite stall. He will bring these trotters home for his sister to boil into a broth, and then he will take the broth to the hospital for his wife.

He steps out onto the footpath, away from the damp smells of the market. This is the suburb of madcap Franco Cozzo and his polished furniture, the suburb that made Russell Crowe rich and famous for shaving his head and beating up ethnic minorities, so it doesn't really matter that these footpaths are not lined with gold but dotted with coruscating black circles where people spat out gum eons ago. "Don't swallow the rubber candy," mothers say to their kids. "Spit it out. Spit it out *now* – that's right, onto the ground there." Ah, this wondrous new country where children are scared of dying because they have swallowed some Spearmint Wrigley's, not because they stepped on a condensed-milk tin filled with ammunition!

So in the beginning it doesn't matter to my father that there may be pee in the pig's blood jelly served in the steaming bowls of *Pho* rice noodles, or that you can't spick da Ingish very well, or that there are certain vegetables you can't get in Tatsing grocery that you could get in Vietnam. No, it doesn't matter at all, because in this suburb he watches grandmas with faces as blunt and brown as earthed potatoes hobble along in their padded jackets. As the wheels of their cloth-covered trolleys roll by, they tell the jabbering children to spit out the gum. My father looks, and smiles, wondering whether his firstborn will be a girl or a boy. He presses the black rubber button on the traffic lights and remembers when they first encountered these ticking poles.

PART I

*H*ERE they all are, standing carefully on the curb at a road crossing – my grandmother, my father, my mother and my Aunt Que. It is early morning, and their grins are so wide that it seems they all went to bed with clothes-hangers shoved in their mouths to save storage space at the Midway Migrant Hostel.

"Wah! Look at that!" cries my grandmother as they meander down the street draped in their De Paul finery, exclusive new arrivals from the St Vincent line. A polyester peasant blouse covers my mother's protruding belly with purple pansies, and she has carefully co-ordinated her white low-heeled pumps with pink Adidas pants. Aunt Que sashays around in a brown dress and a fifty-cent jacket that has real fur on the collar and real mothballs in the pockets. She is followed by my father, sauntering in his fine denim bell-bottoms with brown plastic thongs. He is wearing one of those shirts with the wide flapping collars that point like two arrows at the women on either side of him. Woohoo, look here at my stunning sister and my spectacular wife. Finally, my grandmother pads along in a light-blue cotton pyjama suit she has sewn herself. A pair of sunglasses sits on top of her head – a second pair of eyes gazing skywards, beseeching the Lord Buddha to bless St Vincent and his kind fraternity for vesting the family with such finery.

7

"Wah!" exclaims my grandmother again and points to an old man pressing the squishy black-rubber button. The rest of the gang turn to look. "The cars stopped for that old one!" my grandmother cries. Tic-tic-tic-tic-tic-tic-tic goes the traffic light, and as the green man flashes, the old man casts a suspicious look at the crew pointing at him before hobbling away quickly to the other side of the road.

"Wah!" exclaims my mother. "Look over there! On the other side! The cars even stopped for those little girls!" Two bored ten-year old girls with flouncy balloon skirts sewn to the elastic waistband of their neon biker-pants walk across the road, dappling the bitumen with pastel dribbles from their melting Peters ice-creams.

My father stands in front of the yellow pole and presses the little rubber button again. "Even Mother can do it! Watch me do it again! But try not to gawk like Guangzhou peasants, please." My grandmother ignores the comment and looks up at the lights. "We wait for Mao Ze Dong man to disappear before we move," she instructs. "He stops everything." She is getting the hang of this. As the little Red Man disappears and the little Green Man reappears, the crew hobble to the other side in beat with the ticking traffic light.

Back where my father came from, cars did not give way to people, people gave way to cars. To have a car in Cambodia you had to be rich. And if you had money, it meant that you could drive at whatever speed you pleased. If the driver zipping down the country road accidentally knocked over a peasant farmer, he knew he had better zoom away quick because the whole village might come and attack him with cleavers. The little Green Man was an eternal symbol of government existing to serve and protect. And any country that could have a little green flashing man was benign and wealthy beyond imagining.

*

Wah, so many things about this new country that are so taken-for-granted! It is a country where no one walks like they have to hide. From the top floor of the Rialto building my parents see that the people below amble in a different manner, and not just because of the heat. No bomb is ever going to fall on top of them. No one pissing in the street, except of course in a few select suburbs. No lepers. No Khmer Rouge-type soldiers dressed like black ants prodding occupants of the Central Business District into making a mass exodus to Wangaratta. Most people here have not even heard about Brother Number One in Socialist Cambodia, and to uninitiated ears his name sounds like an Eastern European stew: "Would you like some Pol Pot? It's made with 100% fresh-ground suffering."

Here there is sweetness, and the refugees staying at the Midway Migrant Hilton horde packets of sugar, jam and honey from the breakfast table. So used to everything being finite, irrevocably gone if one does not grab it fast enough, they are bewildered when new packets appear on the breakfast table the next day. So they fill their pockets with these too, just in case. Weeks later, the packets still appear. The new refugees learn to eat more slowly, that their food will not be taken from them or their bowls kicked away. They learn that here, no one dies of starvation.

So in the beginning there are many wahs of wonder, and when my father returns home swinging his bagful of swine hocks, his ears are assailed with even more. "Wah! Look at this

9

water from the tap!" cries my grandmother, handing him a steaming mug. "So clean and hot you could make coffee with it." When they walk to the Western General Hospital with my mother to get the blood tests done, bitumen roads are a source of wonder. "Wah! So black and sparkling like the night sky! Rolled flat by machines and not by stones pulled by a hundred people!" When they catch the tram to declare Australian citizenship, the orderliness of the streetscape does not escape my father, who has proudly memorised all the names of the roads, and in the process the chronological order of this colonised country's monarchs – "King Street, William Street, Queen Street, Elizabeth Street."

My parents become pioneers navigating a new land. Although they travelled through three Southeast-Asian countries by foot, nothing can prepare them for travelling up and down escalators. "Go down!" the rest of my family urge my mother. But she stands firmly at the top, blocking off entry for all other embarkers. She stares down at her husband, her mother-in-law and her sister-in-law, who have already arrived at the bottom. "Ahhh. I'm scaaared!" My father finally steps on, growing larger and larger as he approaches the top with a smirk pasted on his face, like a slow zoom in a cheesy Chinese film. "Just step between the yellow lines," he instructs. "Come on, you've gone up before, so you can come down too! Weeee, wahhh, see what fun!" Up and down and down and up they ride the escalators at Highpoint Shopping Centre – this 32-year-old man, his eight-months-pregnant wife, his 27-year-old sister and the old Asian grandmother in the purple woollen pyjamas. Every journey is one small step for Australians, but one giant leap for the Wah-sers.

The first time my mother walks into a Sims Supermarket, the first moment she sees people loading the trolleys with such habitual nonchalance, she exclaims a long, drawn-out, open-mouthed "wahhhh" of wonder. She would not have been surprised if the baby popped out then and there. This enormous warehouse would shock the eyeballs out of the most prosperous families in Phnom Penh! So gleaming spick-and-span clean! Such beautiful food! Such pretty packages! Packed in shelves so high and deep, all the colours so bright and all the lights so white that she does not know where to look. Aunt Que nudges her: "Ay, stop gawking like such a peasant."

"Wah, you mean *anybody* can come into this big food warehouse?" my ma asks in awe.

"Of course." Aunt Que has only been here once before. "See that fat man with his bumline showing through his shorts? See those little children with no socks? Anybody!" Even the local thong-wearing loiterer can load up a trolley with these treasures, without needing to pause and calculate because it is all so cheap.

As my mother wanders and wonders up and down the aisles, she thinks about being the first in her family to see such magic. She thinks about the ones back in Vietnam. She sees her father sleeping on the floor of the monastery, her mother selling *bancao* at the market. Her skin-and-bones sisters beneath the tap outside with soap powder dripping from their hair. She thinks about the ones back home who are unprocessed and waiting to be processed, unlike the meat that is stacked in tins of twelve in front of her.

"Fifty cents!" exclaims my Aunt Que. "Look, Kien!"

"I know," says my mother, "so cheap, eh? Packed so beauti-

II

fully, too." Back in Cambodia, every canned comestible seemed to have some kind of Lucky This-or-That animal plastered on its label. "Lucky Lion Chilli Sauce." "White Rabbit" candy. "Golden Star Happy Dragon" noodles. My mother looks at my Aunt Que, who is holding a can in her hands and turning it round and round slowly, and she knows that my aunt is thinking of the ones back home too.

"What do you think, Young Aunt?" my mother finally asks. "Should we buy some hah?"

"Yes, let's buy some," determines my Aunt Que. "It's so cheap!"

Back in our rented weatherboard house in Footscray, my mother cuts the meat up into little pieces and makes a nice stir-fry stew. "It smells so good," breathes my auntie as she spoons the meal onto a large plate. My mother cannot help but smile with pride. It is only later when my family sees the television commercial that they realise who – or more accurately, what – the meat is for.

Later that evening, in the bed that fills up the entire small storeroom where they sleep, my mother and father lie thinking about their full tummies. "Wah, who would believe that they feed this good meat to dogs? How lucky to be a dog in this country!" My mother puts her hand on her sticking-out stomach and smiles. Good-oh, she thinks. Her baby is going to be born with lots of Good-O in her. Good stuff.

*

"The hospital nearly gave your father a heart attack when you were born," my mother tells me later. "Your father was at the Migrant Hostel doing his translating job, trying to explain to

12

those countryside Cambodian migrants that the reason that they were so cold in the mornings was because they were meant to sleep *under* the sheets. Their beds were made so nicely when they first arrived that they thought they were meant to sleep *on top* of them. They were scared of mucking up the carefully tucked blankets. No one wanted to be shuffled back onto the plane.

"Your father was trying to tell them that the beds were made to be slept in, when suddenly he was told that he was needed at the hospital. Something must have happened to me, your father thought. Why would a hospital *need* him? He thought about bringing along his acupuncture needles just in case, but there was no time. When he arrived at the hospital, he discovered that the doctors just wanted him to be there to see the baby come out!" In Cambodia the husbands would usually find a chair and sit in front of the room where babies were being born until they heard the wahwahwah sounds, and it was only then that they would know that the whole messy business was over and they could find out whether the child had the desired dangly bits or not.

When my mother wakes up, she notices the white walls, the clean room and the pastel curtains. Just like a bedroom, she thinks sleepily, not a trace of blood or sour meat smell. There are green and red cups of hospital jelly in the tray in front of her, and little dixie cups of vanilla ice-cream. She thinks that the hospital is throwing her a post-birth party. I am the most crumple-faced walnut she has ever seen, and I have a clump of black hair plastered to my head like a Beatle circa the early '60s. This is the one thing the nurses will always remember about me: "She came out with *all this hair* like a little hat!"

they exclaim. "The first Chinese baby we have ever seen, and with a full head of hair!" I keep crying: having unique head-gear obviously does not bring any special consolation. My mother does not know what to do with this little creature with the howling hole in her face; she has been accustomed to me quietly curled up and causing no fuss in her belly, content with whatever liquid morsels passed through her umbilical cord. Now I won't even take my ma's milk. In the end, she feeds me a spoonful of coffee sweetened with condensed milk to shut me up. Only then can she close her eyes and go blissfully back to sleep.

*

"Have you thought of a proper name for the baby yet?" my grandmother asks her son. She has nothing but disdain for those parents who do not give their children Chinese names. Did they really think that new whitewashed names would make the world outside see that yellow Rose was just as radiant a flower as white Daisy?

"I have indeed," says my father. "And not just some common Pretty Pearl or bloody Blooming Orchid name like every second girl!" He holds up a little book with a cover that shows some exceptionally pretty people of all skin tones standing around smiling and patting the heads of catatonic-looking creatures: cattle, lambs and even a lion or two. Written on the cover are the Chinese characters for *Be Ready for the Good News*. Some kind-hearted white folks had given him this free litera-ture guaranteed to put an end to all suffering.

"Good News."

"Good News?" retorts my grandmother.

"Yes, Good News!" claps my father, because this is Paradise, and his baby is born into it.

Next my father has to search for an English name, because his daughter has to have a name that her future legions of white-faced friends will remember, but not a name that she can never grow into. Cousin François is about as French as French fries, French toast and French kiss, while Cousin Candy is more like a piece of congealed toffee stuck at the back of the throat, too gooey to swallow, but too unsightly regurgitated.

Most parents play it safe and stick to the list in the "Naming your Baby" book in the hospital. Yet certain names stand out above the Lin-dahs and the Day-vids of the world. Across the road is a boy named Ao whose father named him after the first half of the Cantonese word for Australia. At the New Star Grocery is a Chinese boy named Freedom, and a Vietnamese girl named Visa. And of course, Richard, for riches. It doesn't matter that Sky will eventually end up working at the bank, that Mercedes will stay in her parents' factory producing picture frames, or that Liberty will get married at eighteen and raise a family of four by age thirty. It doesn't matter that these children will grow up among other playmates whose parents push them so high that their heads spin from vertigo: Day-vid the heart-surgeon by day and hobby concert violinist by night; and young Lin-dah with the lovely brick-veneer double-storey dwelling and a dental clinic above her parents' jewellery store. It doesn't matter, because at this age we do not know that our playmates Lin-dah who used to be Linh and Day-vid who used to be Duong will be jet-setting to their latest holiday destinations in the future with the money earned from their double-happiness salaries, that they will pay with real Visa cards and drive real Mercedes. All this doesn't matter because at the moment they are the ones with the banal unpronounceable names, and we are the children with the special names. We are the ones smiled upon by grown-ups, white people and Fortune.

My father remembers a story translated from English that he read in his youth, about an enchanted land in which a little girl finds herself. This new daughter of his will grow up in this Wonder Land and take for granted things like security, abundance, democracy and the little green man on the traffic lights. She will grow up not ever knowing what it is like to starve. She will go to the Great School, and study to be anything she desires. Then after University, of course she will become a lawyer and marry Day-vid the heart surgeon. "This girl is going to have a good life," says my grandmother. "Look at her now, refusing to eat her congee! Now what child under Pol Pot could have the luxury of refusing food, especially when her mother has carefully sucked the heat out of it in her own mouth first. Ay, this girl is going to have a good life indeed!"

*F*OR Wah-sers like us, there is no such thing as tacky cheap knick-knacks. What an insult to call kitsch all the familiar stuff from the old country, the stuff even wealthy people had in their homes. Baskets for two dollars, colourful pink and red ones, in which to wash the lettuce. Plastic neon-yellow chopstick-holding baskets, plastic racks, plastic bedside tables for thirty dollars each to be assembled at home. Bright prints of Vietnam scenery on shaped plastic to hang on the walls of your house. Colourful floor mats with little animals printed on them. And squeaking sandals for the children, sandals at every corner of the house, so guests do not need to walk around in bare feet. My father brings home twelve pairs of oversized brown plastic sandals that are on sale at a little gift shop in Footscray, where they also sell embroidered slippers for $3.50. Other incense-ridden places in the city or Carlton would sell them for $25.95, under the name of exotic oriental ware.

We are wealthy beyond measure, my father keeps reminding us; not even the wealthy families in Phnom Penh live like this. Some of the furniture given to us by the Brotherhood is better than the furniture for sale in Cambodia. "Ah, look at this house," he laughs as he stands in the front yard of our first home in Braybrook. "It's beautiful! Ah, look at these shoes! I bought them in the largest size possible so they can fit anybody!"

"Not the Aussies," corrects my mother. "Their feet are one and a half times that size!"

"Doesn't matter about the Aussies, they never take off their shoes anyhow."

"Heh heh," laughs my mother, as she stacks my father's brown plastic shoes on a white plastic shoe rack, "a good thing too. Big feet smell."

It is her first house, too, a whole house of her own. Except for the mother-in-law as an unfortunate permanent fixture, it is exactly as my father had promised. My mother buys little glass figurines from the Teochew gift shops that are sprouting up in every street, their racks over-brimming with toilet paper next to plastic flowers next to dog-food dishes next to garish plastic pictures of Jesus Christ with a raised red heart emanating from his chest and rays of fluorescent light reaching to every corner of the frame. "Look at this, Agheare." My mother shows me a small white plastic wheelbarrow with fake flowers spilling out. She places it behind our glass cabinet in the front room of the house for guests to notice. "Beautiful hah?" I agree wholeheartedly. It fits right in with our blue and maroon vase from Uncle Fang's Guangzhou glass factory, and a little white porcelain angel with her features painted too high for the grooves on her face. Beautiful things do not need to be expensive, and precious things are to be kept hidden in case of burglars, or guests with kleptomaniac fingers. My parents could never understand those houses where the Royal Doulton plates and family antiques were displayed for every eye to see. After war, people learn to keep good things hidden. They learn that nothing is permanent, and that the most beautiful things are not necessarily the most expensive.

Grandmother is a collector of string, of Danish biscuit tins, of scraps of paper, and artwork from me. When I come home from kindergarten with bits of macaroni stuck onto a paper plate and spray-painted gold, my grandmother, my auntie and my mother wah over it. How magnificent, they breathe, how precious. No muted tones for us, we like our things two-thousand-decibel colourful. The brighter, the better. At Christmas, when my brother Alexander and I are colouring white paper with crayons to make paper chains because we don't have any pre-printed coloured paper, my grandmother cries, "You silly kids. You don't have to do that, look what I have!" She holds up a handful of junk-mail advertisements. "Look at all the colour here!" She sits on the floor with us, helping us cut up Target advertisements into strips. We make paper chains and string them from every corner of the ceiling, hang them from every doorframe. "Isn't this much better than white paper?"

White is the colour of mourning, red is the colour of blood and life and sunrise, and black is the colour of the evening. But summer evenings here seem pastel, the weather more tame than in Southeast Asia. In fact, everything about this new country seems more contained, hazy like a sort of heaven, no streaks of red or orange or yellow to assail the eye or unsettle the senses.

In the evenings, the windows are open and we go outside and sit in the trailer Dad brought home from the Alcan factory. It is good in the trailer, we make it bang here and there in the wilderness of our front yard, beneath the tall red-purple plum tree. This tree overshadows all the other trees, stretching its branches like extended arms covering the whole front yard and half the verandah, and in between are the smaller trees, the bushes, the ferns clamouring for the light. Red leaves cover the ground of the front yard, and the whole place is like a rainforest without rain. You cannot tell that this is a Chinese house. No hexagonal I Ching mirror on the front door, no words of warning, no clipped hedge and double happiness signs anywhere, unless you count the name of our street. No neat little cumquat trees at the front for luck.

We are trying to assimilate, to not stand out from the neighbours, to not bring shame to our whole race by carrying over certain habits from the old country, such as growing chickens in the backyard or keeping goats as pets. The plants we plant in the backyard are functional plants, herbs like hot Thai mint, basil, shallots and lemongrass, and we have geraniums and oleander in the front yard.

In fact, if you watch from the outside, you will see the crinkle-faced Asian grandmother watering the bird-of-paradise flowers with the hose. Through the back window of the house you will see the mother washing the dishes in the kitchen, and in the front yard you can watch the two children with half-coconut-shell haircuts poking holes in the dirt and trying to plant black custard-apple seeds, and everything seems so true-blue suburban that you would never suspect that the inside of the house is crowded with such a collection of curiosities that make us smile, make my father clap his hands in delight as he peers up at the smiling faces of Ordinary Australians cut up from the Target brochures and strung up in sticky-taped chains in every room.

*

Paper chains and plastic sandals aside, when my mother's two little sisters first arrive and settle into their housing commission flat, I come face to face with what I consider to be true cutting-edge Chinese chic. When they step off the plane, Aunt Ly and her little sister Sim are like those heroines in the movies set in pre-war Shanghai, that big booming city full of newly arrived dowdy women who come with boxy brown suitcases and countryside smiles smeared on their faces, ready to *make it*. They walk with dreams on their heels and the heels of their dreams: spangles, gold lamé and rhinestones, the height of glamour. They wear floating dresses they have made themselves – polyester is silk that requires less ironing, and the colours are infinite.

And when they move into their own flat, they show us that domestic glamour is not confined to the suburbs. The housing commission flats, with their distinctive checkered floors, are better than the apartments in those Hong Kong serials my grandmother watches with my mother, complete with commercials copied direct from HK Television that you have to fast-forward. Those videocassettes are illegally shipped to Australia to stock the shelves of illegitimate video shops or even the lounge-room collections of extended families who pass them back and forth like shared secret pleasures. These serials have twenty-eight, twenty-nine videos and my mother and my grandmother discuss what has happened in them over the kitchen table while peeling carrots and chopping beans because my grandmother is a brilliant storyteller and conversationalist when she is not attacking people with bones in her words.

From the top of the Housing Commission flats you can see down below to the park and the playground equipment – they don't even have such private parks in Hong Kong! These flats have two or even three rooms, a bathroom, and a kitchen with black and white tiles – oh, such class, just like the black and white tiles in the rich people's mansions, except in plastic laminex. Easier to clean, you see.

In the cupboards of those flats are endless cups of coffee and sweetened condensed milk and multitudes of Marmee instant noodle packets. And when it is cold outside it is always warm inside. From the eleventh floor you can see down, and people are always walking in and out of their doorways, so many people so close. Laundry is always hanging outside, and plastic buckets, usually red ones for some bright reason, perhaps to counteract the distinct mossy-seepy smell of stairwells.

My aunts buy nail polish for twenty cents a bottle and sit on the floor of their bedrooms painting their toes. They curl their hair at the flats of their friends who are training to be hair-dressers. Many old folk who became family friends take good care of them, tell them who are the good boys, and the old women watch with a cunning eye to see which young woman would be best suited for the son or cousin of so and so. "Ah Ly, I know a good young man for you." And they sing the praises of someone's son or someone's brother – never mentioned by name, they are always someone's son or someone's male relative, because they do not exist in isolation of their family. No one exists in isolation of their family, and if they do, there are plenty of old people to look after them and plenty of old people to look after, who live in the housing commission flats and whose sons and daughters leave them to mind the house and the babies while they both work to earn enough to raise their children born in the old country or the new.

These young women, proud and beautiful by virtue of being young, smile deliriously so that their cheeks glow and they can take their beautiful faces plein-air into the parks, except they choose to dab on fuchsia pink powder and mascara their lashes. They want to be the Taiwanese singer Teresa Tang, these young women in their Salvation Army stilettos and their fifty-cent lipsticks.

They find many friends, women like themselves at the height of glamour and prime of fertility, and in this country filled with hard-working young migrant men with determination in their eyes and the fire of the same dream burning in their bellies filled with factory working-class diet of two-minute noodles, there is no fear of not finding a family. So trusting, these young women from Southeast Asia, believing that because they are granted these new apartments and these new lives and the government takes such good care of them, that all Australians are alike.

So when my Auntie Ly's friend Ah Ngo needs to make a phone call because she has forgotten the number of Ly's flat, she thinks she can go to any flat door and knock; that all Australians are as kind as the Brotherhood of St Laurence ladies who have given her the dress she is now wearing, white with little brown and blue flowers scattered all over it, a flowing Monroe skirt below the knees and a little matching belt at the waist. So there she is, hair freshly layered and feathered around her face, lipstick on, high-heeled pumps, knocking on the door.

The door opens and she gesticulates hand to ear and smiles and says "Fon, fon?" because she knows that in these flats, the phone is close to the kitchen which is close to the door, and the burly white man in the singlet lets her in. Being Asian, she takes off her shoes at the door, and she goes to the phone and just as she fumbles in her purse for the little slip of paper which has Ly's phone number on it, just as she is about to make her call, head cocked to one side wedging the phone between her ear and her shoulder while she unfolds the little piece of paper, she feels a sharp jab on her behind and it is the Aussie bloke's hands and his front up against her back. The phone drops and she screams and bolts out of there so fast that he is left with a pair of white high-heeled pumps inside his flat, shoes which are too small for any Western woman's feet, and he does not know what to do with them. He picks them up, examines them, looks at the little heels and the plastic bows on the front. Then he peers out the window at the park below and flings them down one at a time, watching them fall to the concrete below. He closes the window and sits down to watch a bit of television.

Meanwhile, Aunt Ly's friend Ah Ngo runs up the flight of stairs because she does not know where to go and to go down would be to go down six more floors and she can't think clearly except to escape and up she goes and up seems like the only direction and in any case, the staircase in front of her goes up and so that is where she goes. She pants and sobs and heaves up the stairs and in the middle, just when she thinks her legs are going to give way, she hears a familiar voice: "Ay, ay, where are you going? I was just going down to look for you," and looks up to see my Auntie Ly and my Auntie Ly can see that something has happened. And so she takes her friend into her flat and she is shoeless but safe. And they both realise that it is not so safe here, and even though you are young and lovely you are not invincible.

M Y mother teaches me to obey my elders, and I grow up with filial piety permeating through every pore, so that when we have dinner with my grandmother, no one ever starts eating until she picks up her chopsticks. My grandmother sits at the head of the table, and I am always seated on her right-hand side. Whenever an unsuspecting soul picks up their chopsticks prematurely, she turns to me. "You know, Agheare, when your uncles and father were small, whenever they picked up their chopsticks before the adults did, or whenever they did not hold their bowls in their hands properly, I would say, 'No manners hah?' and they would plead for me to teach them. 'Ma,' your uncle would say, 'Give me a whack over the knuckles if you catch me doing that again!'" My grandmother loves using this story of my father and his sadomasochistic siblings to prove how well she brought up her children, but after hearing it so many times and seeing my father smile over the table every time, I have my doubts about it.

Next, my grandmother says her version of grace. "Ah, Buddha bless our Father Government," she exults. "Treating us better than our sons do. Giving old people money every fortnight.

"Agheare," she tells me, "when you are old enough and speak the English good enough, you have to write them a letter."

"Yes, Ma."

"In the letter I want you to write how much old people appreciate the money."

"Yes, Ma."

She has a little think about it. "It's so much. Oh, it's all too much, really. I want you to write that."

"Yes, Ma."

"More filial than sons!" cries my grandmother, ignoring my father who is no longer smiling at the dinner table. "Buddha bless Father Government!" She calls it Father Government, like Father Christmas, as if he is a tangible benign white-bearded guru with an everlasting bag of cheques slung over one shoulder. Father Government looked after us when Motherland China didn't want us, and took us in when that angry adolescent orphan Cambodia decided to abandon us to Brother Number One. My grandfather had died under Ah Pot, and my grandmother does not hesitate to adopt a new father for her children: "Father Government looks after all of us so well!"

The only person who does not feel the permeating love of the Father is my mother. Certain people are blocking her way to the light of his everlasting abundance. My grandmother, to whom she hands all her money. And my father, who is still a dutiful son to his mother. So my mother does not make me promise to write any letters to the Father. Instead she sits at the table, penning out her primary-school words in letters to her parents. "Dear Ma. This new country is beautiful. We live in a big house, much bigger than the one belonging to Auntie Mao in Vietnam. Agheare is now two years old. She talks a lot. How is the family back at home? I hope Ba is not still sick. He will be happy here. We will bring you over soon." She cannot write what she really wants to say because my grandmother posts off all the letters, while she is locked in this weatherboard house with thin walls.

"Got any letters that need posting?" my grandmother asks in the early morning. "I am going to the bank, and I am going to take Agheare for a walk." "Willing to walk" is the Teochew term for being filial, and my mother watches as her daughter gets ready to walk off with the other side. She stands at the sink, bubbles from the laundry soaking into her skin. Looking at her daughter, she curls her fingers into the suds, but she is clutching at nothing, just sheets of empty water. Wiping her hands on her blue tracksuit pants, she goes into the room and emerges with her letter.

After my grandmother leaves, she thinks up the letter she really wants to write. At first it comes out as a blur of black cloud, but then words emerge from the smog. "Dear Ma, this family treats me like a servant, like that servant Red Bean that they brought back from China to work around the house and factory in Cambodia." My mother pauses to remember the little servant girl with her shoulders always thrust forward and her face always burning vermilion, like a little red bullet. "Ma, why did you let me go?" she wants to write. My mother feels her own heart is a little red bullet, poking around in her chest, searching for a way out.

*

Lining up at the bank to collect what she calls her "old people's gold", my grandmother searches the faces of all the others standing there with their hands thrust deep in their pockets, and she wonders why they aren't basking in the glow of the

27

glorious government. In fact, a lot of them look as if they have sucked on seven lemons and forgotten to spit out the pips. She smiles at the white-faced, sallow-eyed sad-sacks. "Agheare, these people don't realise what they have. Ah, just like your mother, always shuffling around with that face that looks as if it has been freshly dug out of the morgue!" She feels such love and simple abundance that she decides then and there she will spread good karma around by doing a good deed. After she collects her money, she walks with me to the shop in Footscray which has tanks in the windows and a sign stuck on the glass saying "Fish for food not for pet." She buys a red plastic bucket and a bleary-eyed grey-scaled fish, and we board a bus.

"Ma, what are we doing?" I ask. People on the bus watch as my grandmother sits down and places the bucket on the floor between her feet. She wedges her legs closer together to hold it in place. "We're going to let the fish go."

"Why, Ma?"

"Because Buddha has blessed us! Blessed us!"

The fish is still thrashing around in the bucket, and water is splashing onto her fleecy pants. When the bus passes a little bridge, my grandmother decides that it is time to disembark. Standing at the small overpass bridge, my grandmother heaves the bucket up, onto the edge. "Little fish swim away and have a good life, and Buddha protect you." She turns the bucket upside down. The fish falls into the water with a little plop. More accurately, into the brown diarrhoea sludge of the Maribyrnong.

"Umm, Ma, the water is muddy."

"Doesn't matter, the Mekong is also muddy, and look how many fish they pull out of there every day. Ah, but you wouldn't understand, and lucky for you to be born in this blessed land, you will never see the Mekong where they also pulled out muddy people that didn't move, during the years of Ah Pot! Aiyah, those were terrible years, but wah, Father Government is so good to us now!"

*

When my grandmother and I return from our walk, the laundry is done and my mother is preparing lunch. My grandmother sits at the table and starts counting her Father Government money. Her Father Government money includes the money my father earns because he gives everything to her. "Here is twenty dollars for next week's grocery shopping," my grandmother says. Then she writes down something on a piece of paper. Marking down the exact amount, thinks my mother, making sure I come back with the change. "Make sure you put it in a safe place," says my grandmother. She does not like giving out notes to be broken up. Whenever she goes shopping, she likes to give the exact amount. Getting wrong change can be ghastly if you do not speak the English, so she makes those pasty-faced young people behind the counter wait while she counts out her coins, right down to the brown one-cent pieces.

"When you go shopping tomorrow," my grandmother advises, "try to get that older woman with the dark hair and moustache. I see those young ones looking at one another whenever I come. Young people these days, so impatient. I hope Agheare does not grow up to have that kind of nature."

What kind of nature will her daughter have, my mother wonders the next day, as she shops for the evening's dinner.

What kind of nature, if the girl is always being whisked away from her? *The more people who love her, the better,* my mother reasons as she picks out a cold fish from the market, but her heart cannot cling to reason. In the evening, she watches the family eat the fish she has prepared, the fish that my grandmother lamented cost too much – "Hah, some people don't know how to save money! Could have got a bigger one from the other market for fifty cents less!" My grandmother sits me on the dinner table so I can poke out the fish's eyeball with one chopstick. The eyeballs are my favourite part of the fish. "Like a little demon!" my grandmother claps her hands. The demented red bullet inside my mother's chest tunnels its way in all different directions. It is going ballistic and making holes everywhere, holes in places where no hole should ever be. It is going to drive her crazy, it is going to push itself out and embed itself in her own flesh and blood. She wants this little daughter to be completely her own, but the girl is already doomed. She can see the signs of leaving already, in the glint of her black eyes. Well, my mother thinks, better the girl go to the other side of the Served rather than stay on the side of the servants.

So when the child drops the chopstick, clambers off the table and clutches her leg with icky-fish hands and cries, "Ma! Ma!" the mother turns away. "I'm busy clearing up. Go and bug your grandmother." After all, "Ma" is also the word she uses for grandmother, just two tones different.

FROM a very early age, I know that my grandmother and my mother do not get along. So I become an informer at the age of four, moving from one camp to the other, depending on which side offers the best bribes.

"Agheare, what does your mother say about me when I'm not around?" my grandmother asks me.

"Agheare, what does your grandmother tell you about me?" my mother asks in turn.

I have no sense of loyalty. "Being good" is what each camp demands of me. I find out early that "being good" can mean completely different things. Being good for my mother is telling her what my grandmother says about her. And being good for my grandmother is telling her what my mother says about her. So I discover that being good means just being good to the person who is telling you to be good. Being good is when your grandmother gives you sweets for loitering around the room in which your mother and your third auntie are having a discussion.

"Ah, Samso, don't lament and suffer, because she gave me the same treatment when I first arrived too, except worse," my mother tells my third auntie, who has recently arrived from Guangzhou, China. Clinging to the doorframe, I poke my head into the room.

Soon my mother realises the point of these missions and nudges my aunt, "Eh, Samso, we can't talk any more because she's listening," and they both give me a glare.

I return to my grandmother's room, where she is sitting on the bed waiting for my news, with nothing to report except that my mother and my aunt have stopped talking because they know I am listening.

"Hah!" puffs my grandmother. "That means that they were talking about me! They must have been talking about me!"

I don't understand why they care so much about what each is saying about the other, but I am getting sweets and hair-ties from my grandmother so I don't complain.

And the stories go on. "Your grandmother is trying to turn you against me," says my mother. "She is trying to make you hate me."

"Your mother," my grandmother says, "knows bugger-all about anything. She is so very cruel to a poor old person like me."

"If you do evil deeds," my grandmother tells me, "you will have a bad karma debt, and in your next life you will be turned into a snake or something terrible like that."

"You are so evil," my mother tells me one night, very upset, "that I'm going to take your brother and go away with him. We will go so far far away to a place that you will never find us, and your father needn't bother to look for us because he will never find us either. And you won't ever see us again because we won't be coming back. Ever."

"Ma, please don't go," I beg, feeling the worst kind of sinking fear inside me.

Then it gets as terrible as it can get. "I am going to take

your brother and then I will kill myself and you will never see me again!"

"Ma!" I plead, "please don't go off and kill yourself! I won't be a word-spreader anymore!"

I cannot eat dinner, and that night lying in the bed I share with my grandmother, I cannot sleep either. It is like someone is sitting on my stomach. My grandmother asks me, "What's wrong? Do you need to use the potty?"

"No, I can't get to sleep. My tummy hurts."

"I'll give it a little rub with Tiger Balm oil."

"No, it doesn't hurt that much."

"Then go to sleep."

I lie awake, staring at the ceiling, wondering whether I will hear my mother and my brother get up in the middle of the night. What if they never come back because I am so evil? I decide to stay up so I will be ready when they go. I will hide the keys to the front door. I will put a chair against the back door. I will stand in the way or sleep in the entrance. But with my grandmother rubbing my tummy, I soon drop off to sleep. The next morning, I wake up to find with the greatest relief that they are still there.

"I don't like word-spreaders," my mother tells me. "You have been spreading words again, haven't you?"

"No."

"Don't lie to me."

"I didn't." I am lying, of course, and I know that she knows.

"You told your grandmother that I said she was always wearing those clip-clop shoes to annoy me when I am sleeping. Who could have told her that story? The bloody spirits? I will never tell you anything again, because you are such a word-spreader."

As I sit at the breakfast table, in front of the egg my grandmother has boiled for me, I realise that there is no getting out of this mess. If I stop telling things to my grandmother she will stop loving me, but if I stop telling things to my mother she will stop loving me. On the other hand, if I stop word-spreading to my grandmother, my mother will love me again, and if I stop word-spreading to my mother, my grandmother will love me even more. I always spread my jam on toast all the way to the very edges – no millimetre of bread is left blank and uncovered. My word-spreading habits are similar. There is only one thing left to do, which is to stop talking altogether – but not talking when adults are speaking to you warrants a whack over the head.

The questions become more difficult. "Who do you love more, your grandmother or me?" my mother demands.

"You," I reply.

"You're just saying that because I am asking you. I bet if your grandmother asked you the same thing, you would say her, wouldn't you?"

"No," I lie, but she had and I did.

"Woe, who can trust such a child who lies?" laments my mother. "I can't believe you anymore."

Then she asks again, "Who do you love better, your grandmother or me?"

"You."

"But your grandmother bought you books and those coloured pens the other week." She tries to catch me out.

"You," I reply stubbornly.

*

"Aiyoooo, your mother doesn't even care for her kids," my grandmother says with a tut-tutting of her mouth, "Always out there in the back shed working when she should know that the greatest role of a woman is to take care of her kids." Then my grandmother sighs and shakes her head and tut-tuts with her tongue some more, remembering bringing up eight children, all literate and clean.

"Aiyooo, your mother is always working and doesn't even take the time to realise that you are not even wearing enough warm clothes," laments my grandmother. "Your mother is always in that shed and doesn't even have time to boil you an egg." And so it is my grandmother who wakes up early to boil me the egg, and do my hair into two braids at the top of my head, and bundle me in little padded and patterned Mao suits sent by aunts from Hong Kong.

"What's the matter, Ma?" I ask in panic during the moments I catch my mother staring into nothingness, her eyes glazed and her features blurred. "Nothing," she replies quietly.

"Why are you sad, Ma?" I ask.

"Nothing you would understand. You're still a child."

When I am a bit older, I don't know whether her answer is a lament or curse: "Just wait till you get older and have a mother-in-law like mine. *Then* you will understand. You will understand." What will I understand? I wonder. Suffering? There are far better things to understand than the inconsolable hardships of life. Constantly sighing and lying and dying – that is what being a Chinese woman means, and I want nothing to do with it.

They keep all these secrets, and tell them to four-year olds who cannot possibly understand the complicated channels of hatred, but are meant to keep quiet about such things. I do not understand the loneliness and desperation that would drive a person to find their closest confidante in a toddler more interested in collecting Easter Egg foil.

"Did you know that your grandmother was never the only wife of your grandfather? Did you know your grandfather had two wives at once?"

"Did you know that your mother was not your father's first fiancée?"

"Did you know that your grandfather made your grandmother give away a son?"

"Did you know that your grandmother had two daughters who died in Cambodia?"

Words with bones in them, my grandmother calls them. Words to make the other person fall flat on their back and die a curly death, my mother says. The sharp ones, the ones you can use if ever you need a weapon to protect yourself.

And so I was doomed, early on, to be a word-spreader. To tell these stories that the women of my family made me promise never to tell a soul. Perhaps they told me because they really *did* want the other camp to hear. Perhaps my word-spreading was the only way they could voice their grievances.

Or perhaps my word-spreading is also the only way to see that there was once flesh attached to these bones, that there was once something living and breathing, something that inhaled and exhaled; something that slept and woke up every morning with the past effaced, if only for a moment. That there was a good beginning, and in this good beginning the stories would come like slow trickles of truth, like blood coursing through the veins.

*M*Y grandmother was possessed of healing powers, or so it was claimed by those who knew her back in Cambodia. Five sons, people exclaimed – seven children, all of them so bright! Of course, everyone chose to forget about the first two babies who died, because they were just girls. Back then, with the arrival of each child, she seemed to grow in stature, seemed to loom larger than before, unlike some mothers who turned into wispy-haired waifs after the birth of their third. Children were drawn to her. Wherever she walked, there was always a little one pulling at her trouser leg. "Ma! Ma!" they cried, and they followed her like lambs. She did not shake them off, so they sat at her side while she whirred away on her sewing machine, they crammed into her bed and drenched her clothes with their water-logged dreams. She never told them to piss off, because my grandmother never swore at her children, only at my grandpa.

"Healing powers my bum," my grandpa had scoffed when she told him that because of her powers, she was now the mother of two new boys, one aged seven, the other four. "As if you do not have enough children of your own to look after!" When it came down to childrearing, they were *her* children, he had nothing to do with such prosaic things. Fathers were only there to plant the seeds, it was mothers who did the watering and the fertilising. Of course, the paternal influence would occasionally return to lop off a few leaves for good measure, and smirk for photographs in front of his prize garden, but he made sure to leave immediately afterwards in case the cumquats only glowed orange but were black inside. It was never the pa's fault if the kids went bad.

"You don't understand anything," my grandmother told him, with a slow sad shake of her head. Least of all did he understand how lucky he was. Two streets down from my grandmother's house, and close to the New Market, there was a mother whose two boys lay moaning in bed, drowning in hot and cold flushes. These boys were friends with my grandmother's own boys. This mother came to visit my grandmother, bedraggled with grief. "My boys," she cried, "my boys! Aiyoh, Sister, I need your help! My boys!" They were sick again, but they had always been sickly since they were small. Perhaps it was the air, or the inauspiciousness of their birthdates, but my grandfather suspected they were just spoilt. With every little sniffle attended to, no wonder they liked to slouch around feigning illness.

"Ah Gim, don't worry," reassured my grandmother, with a little pat on her friend's hand. "They will get better, they always do." But from the look in the woman's eyes, she could sense that this time it was worse, this time there seemed to be no redemption.

"The sickness," cried Ah Gim, "they both have the sickness!" The sickness was the smallpox epidemic, for which later every schoolchild had to have their skin scraped with the edge of a knife dipped in ointment. To this day, my mother still bears the scars of the operation on her arm, but Ah Gim's two boys had caught the disease before the immunisation. "I need your help!" cried Ah Gim. "We need to trick the demons into not taking my sons! Aiihh, this is all my fault, for loving them too much and for making it so bleeding obvious!"

There were dour-faced demons everywhere, and these demons were bent on breaking the bond between mothers and their children. These demons were also gods that needed to be appeased – or deceived if that did not work. Oh, they were insatiable, and to deceive these demons, mothers would try to confuse them, forcing their own children to call them "Aunt" instead of "Ma". "From now on, I am your auntie," Ah Gim commanded, standing in front of her two boys. "From now on you must call me Aunt. Do you understand?"

Her poor pale-faced children blinked up at her from their beds. "Don't give me that confused look, stupid squids, this is for your own good." Then she turned her face with her chin thrust up high towards the firmament, or wherever she thought the demons were floating. *What, me tormented? You've got to be kidding. I'm just the aunt, these are not my kids, take them if you want, I don't want them. In fact, if you take them, you'd be doing me a favour, I'm sick of looking after these phlegmy princes anyhow.*

But the children could not be orphans, either, because to be an orphan was to be the saddest kind of soul in the world, for without a beginning, the ending was bound to be swift. So this is how my grandmother came to be standing by the foot of their mattress on the floor, looking down at the two boys. They looked terrible.

"Look here, you two. You remember Auntie Huyen Thai?" demanded Ah Gim. The boys stared up at my grandmother, wide-eyed from their illness. Their faces were splotched with angry pink.

"If you don't remember Auntie Thai, then you'd better remember her now, because she is now your mother and you have to call her Ma. Not me. Do you understand?"

The youngest boy's eyes flickered open in panic. Poor kid, my grandmother thought. His sick mind wasn't up to these genealogical gymnastics.

"Call her Ma," commanded their real ma. "She has special powers and will make you better."

My grandmother wanted to open her mouth and protest, but then she saw the look in the other woman's eyes and remained silent.

"She has five sons, born one after the other, and all of them healthy and good …" Ah Gim choked a little on the end of this sentence, because she was looking at her own two boys, "and I have you two sick worms! Sick and useless and causing me nothing but a constricted heart!" She clutched her chest with closed fists, as if trying to hold her ribcage together, and her face twisted up.

"Sister, oh, sister, don't cry," said my grandmother, "it will all be alright. You will see. Your boys will get better. You will see."

Ah Gim's shoulders heaved. Her two boys looked up at her, and then at my grandmother. They didn't know what was going on, and their heads lolled from side to side. "Ma, ma ma ma," they bleated in every direction, like little goats, and their bleats drowned out the sound of their mother's weeping.

So that was how my grandmother came to be in possession of two extra sons, although they lived at the house around the corner. Their "auntie" took such good care of them that my grandmother only had to pay occasional visits. Eventually, the boys did recover from their illness, and although convalescence was slow and their faces were to be permanently cratered, their mother declared it a miracle. She dressed them in their best white shirts and trousers ironed so neatly that the creases in the middle could cut fingers, and she sent them to my grandmother's house. "But we don't want to go, Auntie," they protested.

"Must go," demanded their mother.

"But Auntie …"

"Must." She turned her face away from the boys as a smile crept onto her face. She thought that she had put one over the gods.

"Our auntie sent us here to call you Ma," said the seven-year-old boy tentatively, standing in the living room of my grandmother's house. My grandmother sat in her brown wooden chair, looked closely at the two spotty-faced boys, and beamed. "So good to see that you boys are all better now!" she cried. "Oh, I am so happy!"

My grandfather, who was sitting opposite, did not say anything. Ah Gim stood behind her boys, her hand so heavy on each one's shoulder that they appeared lopsided. "Your wife is so clever!" she burbled. "She sure knows how to bring up children, doesn't she? Ah, look at your boys, so good and clever! I only hope that they can be a good influence on these two useless ones."

Not knowing how to answer, my grandfather decided to resort to his repertoire of grunts and hmmmpphhs, from which it was impossible to tell whether he concurred or was contemptuous. He scarcely glanced at the two boys and their overzealous aunt. He bore the agony of this visit only by reading a thin volume of Mao Ze Dong poems. Finally, it was time for them to leave.

"You must bring your sons over to play one day!"

"Of course! Of course!" said my grandmother. She was standing up, ruffling the hair of the two boys as they walked towards the door.

"Now say goodbye to your ma!"

The two boys dutifully bleated their farewells.

*

When my grandmother returned to the room, my grandfather was still reading. "Two new sons, now," said my grandfather, as he slowly turned a page, "two new sons. Are you planning to adopt any more? Perhaps a few more daughters from the village. Yes, a few more girls from the village and perhaps a little goat too hah?"

"What is the matter with you?" demanded my grandmother.

"Oh, nothing, nothing."

"You should be happy. The more children the merrier."

"Hmmmpphhh," muttered my grandfather, "they're not my children."

"Ah! So that's what it is, is it?"

My grandfather remained silent.

"Not my fault that children like me," said my grandmother.

Finally my grandfather erupted. "Sure, children like you, even pockmarked poor excuses like that. But let me tell you one thing. I think you should take care of your own children before your fingers begin to itch for anyone else's."

"What's that supposed to mean?"

"Exactly what I said."

"And what have you said, old man? Stop talking in circles and tell me what you're getting at."

"Well," began my grandfather deliberately, "I thought you had no interest in sons, considering what you were trying to do with our fourth boy."

"Fourth boy was the past!" cried my grandmother. "How could you still go on and on about that, reciting past wrongs like a Buddhist mantra!"

"Indeed," scoffed my grandfather, "bundling up our baby like that and setting off to sell him for a useless daughter!"

My grandmother sighed. "Ah, when will you ever forget that?"

"Never! You tried to swap our son for someone else's daughter! I should have given you a thrashing! Trying to get rid of a healthy boy!"

The entire story was true, my grandmother was ashamed to admit, but it was also true that she pined for daughters above all else. "I did it for the money," she had cried when my grandfather found out. "After all, daughters are easier to feed!"

"Such shame on our family if anyone were to find out what crazy things my wife does!" railed my grandfather, wishing my grandmother was an uneducated country girl instead of this strong-jawed communist.

"Well, I got him back!"

"After making me lose so much face you might as well paint a new pair of eyes on my neck!"

*

My grandfather had stopped living with my grandmother after the birth of the fourth son. He had two wives, and returned to his first. The first wife was a marriage arranged by his father. Marrying for love was a luxury, yet when he met my grandmother he could afford few luxuries in his life, being a teacher with two daughters to support. But he did it anyway. And now he wondered whether he had any regrets, whether what he did was a wise thing, considering the crazy things this second wife did. Yet he did not doubt that any child my grandmother took on as her own ended up being obedient to her, filled with such filial piety and respect that they became members of her little army. His sons obeyed him because they were afraid of him, but they followed her because she commanded them. The children seemed no longer theirs, but hers alone, for she alone held power over them.

He did not like this.

My grandfather saw that after her third son was born, people began to look at my grandmother with more respect. After her fourth, with admiration. After her fifth, with awe. "So blessed Huyen Thai is!" Then, when it came to her sixth, it was too much. She bore too much luck and success. The five sons were making her powerful beyond the understanding of my grandfather. She controlled these five little boys who were going to grow into men, and it made my grandfather anxious. They did exactly as she told them. She taught them songs about the homeland, China of course, the communist homeland. The Motherland. "One day I will send you all back," she vowed, "to become Chinese. This barbarian land is crazy. We have a moonfaced maniac prince who stars in his own movies while there is a civil war going on!"

So when my grandmother was pregnant with her sixth son, my grandfather made a plan to recruit his own army. She was getting too powerful, this woman, with too many people calling her "Ma" this and "Ma" that.

"Tell us a story, Ma!" cried my three-year-old father, "tell us a story!" And tell them stories she did, with each character coming to life as she stretched her face and contorted her mouth, furrowed her brow and brought to life people she liked and people she loathed to battle it out between the heaven and the earth. My grandfather suspected that she made him into one of the characters, perhaps the main one, the main foe with the ferocious face and the ability to startle little children into peeing on the bed.

Back in his first house things were not so interesting. His first wife could not tell stories, at night she went to bed early, and she slept with her mouth dry and open. His two daughters were dull things, they were good and obedient and took in sewing work at home, but they lived to see themselves married where their obedience and goodness would be better appreciated. It was more peaceful in this house than in the house of his second wife, if peace could be defined as absence of ammunition. Of course, there were short sporadic bouts of open fire, when the thought of the second wife was too much for first wife to bear, but my grandfather had a simple and effective way to silence these remonstrations: "If you could give me sons, then I wouldn't need to go over there!" In the end, he thought of a way to put a stop to all his problems, an ingenious way to shut up first wife and make that supercilious second wife learn a little humility. Of course, like all his plans, whether they came into fruition ultimately depended on my grandmother, and this irritated him no end, but there was nothing else for it.

*

"You have to help me!" cried my grandmother, banging on the wooden door to Ah Gim's house. "Help! Help! Thief! Robber!"

When Ah Gim opened the door, my grandmother charged inside and slammed the door. Standing with her back against the doorway, she heaved and choked, her face the colour of taro, a nebulous grey-pale-purple. "Lowliest scummiest lowlife mugger in the world!"

"Sister, sister, what is the matter? Who robbed you? Was it at the market? Where is your handbag?"

"Handbag?" My grandmother stared at Ah Gim as if she were the hysterical one. "Handbag! Hah! She thinks it's my handbag! Yes, a handbag I have been carrying for nine months!" Her eyes rolled towards the ceiling, and then back towards her friend, focusing for the next outburst. "He took my son! He took my baby!"

"Wah! Woe!" cried Ah Gim, "Who? When? How did it happen? Did you see his face?"

"Of course, I know every speck on that no-good face. It was my husband!"

"Your husband! Where did he take your son?"

"To the Other Side!" shrilled my grandmother. "He took my son to the Other Side! Oh, he had this planned for so long! He was waiting for the boy to be weaned, he was waiting with his eyes glinting and his hands itching!"

Her friend stood there helplessly. Clutching the sides of

46

her trousers with tight hands, she wailed, "But sister, what can I do?" She was one for commiseration, not action, one who waited for others to save her.

"We're going over to his first wife's house and we're going to snatch my boy back!" It was not a request, it was a command.

"Aiyah, oyah ..." Ah Gim lamented. Somehow the presence of this woman cast a dark shadow over her own small selfhood, made her aware of her ineffectuality.

My grandmother grabbed Ah Gim's wrist. "Now!"

Ah Gim had to obey, she had no choice, she was led by her guilty sense of gratitude and my grandmother's powerful tug.

But the tug was not strong enough, for they came back empty-handed.

*

How did that happen? I often wonder. How could someone like my grandmother bear to have her baby given away? The alternative I cannot fathom – that it would have been an arrangement, and that she would have known during the pregnancy. Yet characters are only fixed through experience, and usually bad experience. Before character there is only personality, and who knows what kind of person my grandmother was back then?

Yet one thing I know for certain. He was never snatched back, that last son. Fast-forward fifty-five years, and a man from Macau appears at her funeral. He is very short with a gentle face. He was never snatched back – you can tell because he looks into the glass of her coffin without the same solemnity as the rest of my uncles. Why was my grandmother unsuccessful at stealing her son back? Perhaps she just learned to let him go. After all, there would be more children. There would always be more children, to cling to her pants-legs, to ask her about maths problems, to make paper chains with, and to share her big soft bed.

"Tell me a story," I would plead, snuggling up to my grandmother in her bed. My grandmother always had a queen-sized bed in Australia. "Tell me a story." And there would be stories such as I had never known, could never tell, and will never know again because my grandmother was possessed of a form of magic, the magic of words that became movies in the mind. The people she spoke about came alive through her voice, her pauses, her animated eyebrows, and the distinction between reality and fantasy no longer had any force. There *was* no distinction, and in the safety of the blankets, all past children no longer mattered. I was her one and only, and I would never have to find out about the one who was given away.

PART II

"WOE," cried my grandmother, "why do you smell like piss?" My grandmother alternated between "Wah!" and "Woe" to express extremes of emotion.

"I pissed my pants."

"Why didn't you tell the teacher you needed to go to the toilet?"

I shrugged and shifted about uncomfortably. Foreign words did not seem to slip out of me as easily as the contents of my bladder, but I knew my grandmother would keep quiet about this. She would protect me from prying parents and their ability to turn my humiliation into an after-dinner anecdote.

*

It was kindergarten photo day and I had been bundled into my pale-blue padded Mao suit with the frog fastenings. Underneath, my grandmother had made me wear my flannel pyjama top and thermal tights. All this clothing made my arms stick out from my sides as if I were a penguin. It was spring Down Under, but my grandmother lived in constant fear that I would freeze like the communist peasants from the Middle Kingdom she had left over half a century ago. My hair was tied with two red ribbons on top of my head, and pulled so tightly that my ears almost met at the back of my head.

"Go down the slide, Alice," coaxed the teachers, "go on!" Terrified, I could not move. I knew that if I were to go down the slide I would leave behind wet streaks of incontinence. The teachers wondered what was wrong with me. The photographer was waiting with his camera. I shook my head.

The swings, perhaps? But I refused to move. I pointed indoors. I went indoors and stayed in there for the rest of my photographs. I stayed there for the rest of the day, doing the only thing possible for me to do standing up.

When the photos were developed, my parents proudly proclaimed, "Ah, look! We have an artist in the family!" My kindergarten album was filled with pictures of me standing next to the easel in a Raggedy-Ann smock, smiling at my own ingeniousness.

That night, in my grandmother's queen-sized bed, she quietly asked me, "Do you *know* how to tell the teacher you need to go to the toilet?"

I nodded. I did.

"Then why didn't you tell the teacher?"

"I don't know," I confessed. But I did know. Fear.

There was silence. I thought my grandmother was asleep. I stared at the gold ring on her hand that was around my shoulder. Then, just as I was about to drift off to sleep too, she suddenly asked, "Have you gone to the potty yet?" My grandmother kept a little tin pot in the corner of the room for both of us to use.

"I don't *need* to go."

She made me go anyway.

When I came back, she waited until I had snuggled into my characteristic cocoon-shape before she spoke.

"In the past in the Golden Towers," my grandmother began, and I knew she was going to tell me about the other country where everybody lived a life before me. All her stories began with things in the past, in Long Mountain, China, or Cambodia, the Golden Towers. "In the past," she said, "when your father was small, we had a mattress, one and a half metres wide, two metres long. Your First Uncle, your Second Uncle, your Third Uncle, your Fourth Uncle and your father – all very small then – all crammed onto the mattress with me. In the middle of the night one by one they would go shhhhhhhhhhhhhh" – she paused for the cocoon to giggle – "and I would wake up with my clothes dripping wet. The mattress would be soaked too, with that slightly minty smell of urine." So *that* was how she could detect piss from metres away. She told me that she was glad I didn't have a night-time bladder. But she made me promise to learn that dreaded foreign sentence so that I would be able to make some friends. Before I drifted off to sleep, I wondered doubtfully whether my "escoose mi plis I nid to go to da toylit" outburst would persuade the other kids to share their Play-Doh with me.

It was not the last time I would refuse to speak, and my pants were filled on a number of later occasions. After the first time, I knew not to tell. My grandmother always found out anyway. It was not the end of the Mao suit, either. In Grade Two, when we studied Australian History, the teachers decided to have a colonial dress-up parade. That morning I rummaged through our wardrobe for a dress long enough to reach my ankles. The wardrobe had been kindly donated by the good St Laurence. My parents had vowed to pay alms to His Brotherhood one day, when they had enough money. But I knew that as kind as the Christians were, there was no chance that this cupboard would contain an ankle-length dress for me. My mother stood behind me watching the futile search. The Mao suit came out.

*

"Why are you wearing your pyjamas, Alice?" toffee-scented, doe-eyed, dimple-faced Kylie asked me. Loud enough for the other girls lining up in swirly floor-length dresses to hear.

Miss Higgins was cutting out crepe-paper aprons for all the girls. I had lined up too. I was the only girl in the line wearing pants. When it was my turn, Miss Higgins looked me up and down. Then came the inevitable words: "No, Alice, I don't think you need one."

The parade was due to begin in half an hour. I would be the only girl without a dress, without an apron! I *needed* that apron. I needed it to cover my pyjama bottoms. What would I do without it? I had no choice. Miss Higgins was getting impatient, the girls behind were getting impatient because I would not get out of the way. I had to ask. But what if she refused me again, as she refused the apron? Yet I knew I had to ask, and there was no getting out of it.

"Excuse me, Miss Higgins." My voice sounded small and ridiculous, like a cannon firing rubber squeaky toys. Yet I had promised my grandmother again and again that I would do it. And I had failed her every time. Instead of bringing home friends, I brought home soiled washing. Now was my chance to make her proud.

Miss Higgins looked expectantly at me.

"Please, Miss Higgins, I need to go to the toilet."

54

"QUICK, it's getting away!" My eyes followed the moving speck. My forefinger pressed down. The enemy was wounded, then pulverised.

"Look, here's another one!" Outside Ma yelled. "Quick, press it! Press it till it pops!" Her fingertip transferred the tiny dot from the wooden comb onto the Target clothing ad. It crawled across the remains of old allies – casualties of the war raging in the dense jungle on my head.

Crushed, it left a skid mark on the page like the flicker of a red biro, in the exact spot where the Model Child with the marble-eyes and $12.99 frock had her nostrils upturned. "Look, Ma, I've given her a blood nose!"

"That's disgusting, stop mucking around." Outside Ma ran the fine-toothed comb through my hair, twenty strands at a time. "Keep your head still."

I was at Outside Ma's house because no other relative would have me over because of my nits. Outside Ma was my mother's mother. Outside Ma did not ask me whether the kids at school were still playing with me. She did not ask whether I was being teased. Outside Ma's questions mostly revolved around bodily functions – "Is your stomach full yet?" "Are your hands and feet cold?" "Is your head itchy?" "Is your nose blocked?" Then she would set about relieving our ailments. Food for the tummy, socks for the feet, gloves for the hands, a fine-toothed nit comb for the hair, and mouth for the nose. I always avoided the last remedy. When my brother Alexander was a baby and had congested nasal passages, I watched Outside Ma suck the snot from his nose with her mouth and spit it into the sink. "That's disgusting!"

"He's only a little baby," Outside Ma muttered. "How do you expect a little baby to blow his nose? He hasn't learned to yet, so I do it for him."

"Aaarghhh! That's sick!" I cried, fleeing from her.

*

When the immigration papers were finally processed, my other set of grandparents had arrived at Melbourne airport in their homemade cotton Mao suits of dark blue and earth-brown. My Outside Grandparents.

My mother recognised them immediately as they came out of the airport terminal. "Ay, ay! It's Ma!" she cried. "It's Pa!" She stood there, face to face with her parents. She touched her father on the sleeve. "New travelling clothes!"

"Your mother made them just before we left," my outside grandfather said, grinning his toothless grin.

"You should see the clothes that you will get here!"

"YiMui," my outside grandmother said to her second daughter, "you've grown fatter." My mother was a couple of months pregnant with my brother Alexander, and still only forty-seven kilos.

"I'm having a baby, remember?"

"Where is our first baby grandchild?" demanded my outside grandmother. Then they saw me.

"Wah! That's not a baby!" exclaimed my outside grandfather. "How old is she now?"

"Almost three."

"So big!"

I was just festively plump.

"This is your Outside Grandmother," my mother instructed me. Outside because my mother had married into my dad's family.

"How are you, Outside Ma?"

"Wah, how clever!"

Funny how adults found certain things clever. Carefully peeling gum from the bottom of the plastic airport-lounge chairs and popping it in my mouth wasn't clever, but repeating four stupid words was.

That day, all my grandparents could do was look – wah, lights at the airport in the daytime were so bright, how did they get them to be so bright? Amazing. And faces were so fat! They had never seen a bunch of more beautiful people in their lives. They took it all in with their wide-open eyes, and ignored the white ghosts floating in their peripheral vision. These people in front of them were the people who mattered, these faces were the faces of the family.

My mother could not stop her hands from moving. She pointed, she jabbed, she spoke at a hundred miles an hour. How happy they all were, and how happy my mother was to see her parents. Everything was so bright and big to my outside grandparents, how much she would have to teach them. Supermarkets. Moving stairs in glass buildings taller than anything imaginable. Hospitals where it was all white inside and like those hotels for Westerners back in the old country. She would show them how they would get a house here even bigger than any of the houses in which they had ever lived in Vietnam or Cambodia. How the government would give them money. "Every Thursday," my grandpa would later hoot almost with tears in his eyes because of bewilderment at the generous whims of the government. "The government gives me money and not only that, when I am standing at the counter, they say 'thank you' to *me*, a useless old man!"

But Grandpa proved to be far from useless. When he and my grandma moved to their own house in Springvale, Grandpa turned his whole suburban back lawn into a ploughed field of brown parallel lines. He dug deep complicated irrigation channels and collected rainwater in big barrels. And in his field he planted Chinese vegetables, flying dragon plants, four types of hot basil, turnips, melons, potatoes, chives, cumquat, plum and lemon trees. At eighty-four he got up at six every morning to water his plants and plough his field, with the bottoms of his homemade polyester-blue pyjama pants rolled up. Meanwhile, Outside Ma continued to sew her Mao suits, right down to the cloth-covered buttons. She even made underwear, with a little pocket on the back just like jeans. They did not trust banks to stay solvent, even during peace-time, so they buried their money in Nescafé jars all over the backyard.

*

I was glad that Outside Ma did not ask me why I had chosen to come to her house that day. I was glad she did not ask why we didn't come over to her house more often. I was glad that she did not ask any of these questions, because then I might have had to tell her the ugly truth: that Alexander and I were there only because no one else wanted us.

*

"We're going to William and Joanne's house!" my five-year-old brother squealed, excited to the point of near-incontinence. After much begging and pleading we had finally been allowed to spend the afternoon at Aunt Meili's. Aunt Meili was my parents' family friend and she lived in a big birthday-cake of a house in Keilor, with an unused dishwasher ("to save water"), plastic coverings on the dining table ("to save table") and a gold lion statue in the hallway near the front door ("to save money").

My mother stalled our Toyota in the street, noticing that Aunt Meili's silver Volvo with the numberplate "WANG88" (the eighty-eight for good luck) was not in the driveway. "Aunt Meili is not home," she said slowly. "I'll take you to your Outside Ma's."

"Just because the Wang Car is not home doesn't mean that William and Joanne aren't home!" pleaded Alexander. "Let's ring the doorbell and see!"

Thirteen-year-old Joanne opened the door. "Oh," she said.

"I am just leaving them here to play," said my mother. "You know how they plead and clamour!"

"Oh," said Joanne, "oh. Okay." She let us in but, strangely, turned and walked away down the hall, back into her room. We heard her door slam. We stood there like sticks. We did not know what to do. Finally, Alexander and I walked into the lounge room and sat on the sofa. We waited for William. We waited. And waited. And waited. Joanne peered in through the sliding glass door. "Where's William?" I summoned up the courage to ask.

"He's in his room," Joanne told us. It was clear that he did not intend to come out. I felt heavy. I slunk back. "Hey, don't lean on the sofa!" Joanne scowled. I forced myself to sit up straighter so that my back didn't touch the leather, and so did Alexander.

Suddenly and unexpectedly, William emerged. Woohoo, I thought, saved! I wanted to clap. William would relieve the boredom! He came towards us. I was just about ready to offer him a standing ovation when he reached past me to grab his transformer toy from the sofa. "Hey, get the clothes off the sofa too!" commanded Joanne. William pushed the half-folded fresh laundry on the sofa into a basket, disappeared into his mother's bedroom with the basket, and then went back into his own room with the transformer, the door slamming behind him. Satisfied, Joanne retreated to her room.

Suddenly I *knew*. It was the nits. Somehow they had found out that we had nits. Occasionally a head emerged from the white blanks of their doorways to check up on us, accompanied by an order – "Don't lie your head on the armrest!" or "Don't sit like that!"

Defeated, Alexander and I knew there was no way to remain on the sofa and not offend our precocious prison wardens, so we slid ourselves onto the floor. There was nothing for us to do. I ran my fingers through the dark pink carpet with the patterned rivulets running through it like scars and wondered what Joanne and William were doing in the lolly-coloured depths of their rooms. The Venetian blinds were drawn, and the entire lounge room was haunted by pinky-purple shadows.

Wish I had my book, I thought. During our epoch on the floor, my brother and I did not speak to each other. "Let's lie on the floor and spread our army over their perfect carpet!" I wanted to tell him. "Come on, come on, I command you to do it!" I imagined a whole army emerging from the guerrilla turf of our black heads, spreading across the veins of the carpet like little white ants, to conquer this new territory. Two by two, ten by ten, three thousand by three thousand they would march, invigorated by the generous sustenance bequeathed them by my personal Blood Bank, and they would spread to every terrain in this Brave New World where everything was pale-pink.

Eons passed with each eye-blink, and we weren't killing time – the time was killing us. When we finally heard the sound of the doorbell, we were off the floor in a split-second. We bolted towards the door with the cooties on our heads clinging for dear life.

*

In the car going home, Alexander and I didn't howl, let alone speak to each other. My mother looked at us and said, "You two look exhausted. I told you not to play too hard! Now you won't have any appetite for dinner!"

She was right. We didn't. I turned to Alexander. His hand went up absentmindedly to scratch his head. That did it. "Don't play with Richard anymore, okay?" Richard was my best friend Beatrice's kid brother. It was the only order I could issue to my five-year-old brother. He nodded. I looked at him and knew he was already intent on avoiding Richard. We were in this together, I realised. I knew that at school on Monday my brother and I would be together at recess and lunch. Just the two of us. And I knew that Beatrice would have to go back to hanging around with her kid brother too. I sank back in my seat with a despair deeper than tears.

"Ay!" came my mother's voice from the front of the car, "don't do that! Do you want the car to be swarming with nits?"

*

"This will kill them all off," said my mother, but it was a lie.

When my mother had finished applying the treatment to my hair, it reeked of fetid alcohol. It was to be left in for another twelve hours, which meant that I had to go to school smelling like cat-piss. "Everybody will know!" I protested, even though I knew that they already knew anyway. "Nonsense," said my father. "Look at how nice and shiny your hair is. People will just think you freshly shampooed it."

But the bottle treatment didn't work.

*

"*Ta ku le,*" said the hairdresser to my mother in Mandarin when my parents came to pick me up. *She has been sooking.*

"No other kid gets twenty-five dollars spent on their hair!" scolded my mother as she led me from the garage salon of the hairdresser to our car. "You don't know how lucky you are. And if the heat from the rollers has not burnt them all dead, then I don't know what will!" She examined the tight poufy little half-loops on my head. "This is much nicer than the scraggly few strands you were growing and brushing. I don't know why you are sooking, honestly. Now don't show that

62

dug-out-of-a-coffin-face when you arrive at Outside Ma's house or else you'll be dead!"

In the car, I despaired. I was Chinese Ronald McDonald, minus the Happy Times. "So curly, so cute," said my father. They were not curls, I decided. I had a perm. No other kid at school had a perm – they had waves, or crimps, or even curls. But not a perm.

When our car arrived at Outside Ma's house, I sat firmly where I was. I did not want Outside Ma to see that our crusade with the comb was in vain. "What do you think you're doing in the car?" cried my mother. "Fermenting? Get out now!"

When I stepped inside Outside Ma's house, I threw a tantrum. I howled on the carpet of Outside Ma's lounge room, my head on the ground and my skinny arms and legs flailing like matchsticks trying to self-ignite on the floor. I howled with my mouth stretched into the gaping sign of infinity. I howled for the loss of my hair. I howled for the lost afternoon spent on the floor of Aunt Meili's house. And finally, I howled for the loss of Beatrice, the best friend I ever had. Outside Ma did not care whether my head was on her carpet, whether my hands were shredding the wool, whether my feet were kicking her sofa. She looked at my mother. "Why is she crying? Is she hungry?"

"A N electrical appliance store? What are you – crazy?" my grandmother cried. "What do people here in Footscray want from a little electrical appliance store? What they really need is another Asian Mixed-Goods store."

"Every Lee and Lah are opening bloody grocery stores!" retorted my father. "You just watch – there will be a grocery store on every corner five years from now. And who wants to go around selling soy sauce and force-fried meat forever?"

So my father, my Uncle Suong and two friends from the Alcan factory decided to form a partnership. The first store that they bought was on Barkly Street, a tiny four-by-five shop with no toilet. Every time my pa needed to relieve himself, he would have to stick the hand-written "BAcK In TeN MInUTEs" sign across the glass door, lock up and pop over to the restaurant across the road.

There weren't many electrical appliances – mainly watches, batteries, little radios and musical Christmas cards. Theft was common, and so was badgering by gangs who came to torment small shop-owners, asking for money – and they wouldn't leave until they got it. "Just like in Cambodia," my father would mutter. "Except now it's not the government officials bugging us, it's these gangs!"

One shop-to-shop supplier would sell adaptor plugs at a

very cheap price. Every time he visited he wore a black leather jacket, and his face was like a potato – dotted with pockmarks. Carrying his goods in cardboard boxes under his arm, he would sit the boxes on the counter for my father and Uncle Suong to sift through. "Great plugs, eh, so much cheaper than buying them from the wholesalers!" exclaimed my Uncle Suong.

Later my father realised that they were *too* cheap and decided not to buy any more. Next time Jacket Potato came, my father said to him, "Sorry brother, we don't need any more of these plugs." He had to start out polite, because he was scared that Jacket Potato would come later with his gang and trash the store.

"Hah?"

"We don't need any more plugs at the moment, brother."

"Nonsense. Everybody needs these plugs. How do you expect people who buy their rice cookers from Vietnam to connect them to the Australian sockets, eh?"

"Tell me something," began my father with studied naivety, "hmm, how do you make a profit hah, with your prices so cheap?"

"What do you mean, my prices are too cheap?" demanded Jacket Potato. "Prices are meant to be cheap, brother. I pride myself on not ripping off the small shop-owner."

"But, your prices are *too* cheap, if you know what I am saying," my father said very slowly, casting a look at my uncle, who nodded. Jacket Potato decided it was no use feigning no-know. "Heh heh," he said, "heh heh brother. I know what you are thinking. And let me tell you, brother, I came from Vietnam two years ago. Back in Vietnam my parents had a little table at the market-place where they sold this and thats to make money, heh. So I assure you, brother, that I only take from the very big stores, you know."

"Big stores?" My father looked at the box of goods in front of him.

"Heh, come on, you know the big stores, brother. Like Kmart. I support small business, brother, I don't do the small stores, you understand. I know what it is like for the small store-owners with the gangs roaming around giving you trouble."

"But … how do you do it?"

"Heh heh, a master never reveals his tricks. But since we are good business partners, let me show you. Let me show you how this master does his tricks, heh?"

"Err, no, it's alright, you don't have to." My uncle looked a little uneasy. My father looked even more uneasy.

"No, no, let me show you how I do it. You are my good brothers, and I will reveal to you what I reveal to no one. Just to show you that I don't do the small stores, even though it is so easy for me to. You can trust me, brothers, eh?"

My father's curiosity got the better of him. "Alright."

So Jacket Potato idly roamed around the tiny four-metre-by-four store, while from the counter my father and my uncle watched his every move. At last when the guy came back, my father said, "But you didn't take anything! Is this a trick?"

"Heh heh, but I did. Man, the master is good." Beneath his jacket he revealed a small clock radio from one of the shelves on the wall. My father and my uncle were slack-jawed.

"How did you manage to do that? We never noticed! We didn't even realise anything was missing!"

"Heh heh," said the man happily. "I told you, brothers, the master is good."

"Wah, how clever you are," said my father with a mix of admiration and trepidation. But from then on, he made sure that we ordered all our plugs legitimately, and half a year later he told Jacket Potato we could no longer order from door-to-door suppliers because we were now a Retravision franchise.

*

Because my father owned a business, in school forms I could fill in "Manager" on the line that said "Father's Occupation". In different times and places, that line could have read factory overseer, wartime acupuncturist and barefoot doctor, Midway Migrant Hostel translator, fruit picker, Royal Melbourne Institute of Technology gold and silver-smithing student, or welder at the Alcan factory.

In the line that read "Mother's Occupation", my father filled in "House Duties", since "Outworker" did not sound too good and might get the authorities coming over to check on us.

The sparks from her kiln in the darkness of the candlelit garage flew like fireworks when my mother worked late into the night, the noise was like thunder and a thousand muffled cymbals. When my father abandoned his plan to open a jewellery store, my mother had already taken over his goldsmithing work. She learnt from watching my father connecting the little links of chains together, firing up the kiln and filing down rings. Many mornings I would wake up to the smell of wax – the wax came from a machine that squirted it into rubber jewellery moulds. These rubber moulds were hand-cast by my parents. My father would sandwich a real ring or pendant between sticky pieces of special rubber that were cut to fit snugly into little metal frames. Then he would put the frame into the kiln. When

67

it was taken out, the adhesive rubber sheets melted into a rubbery mould. Using a razor blade, my father would slowly and carefully cut the ring from the mould and remove it.

My mother would then fill the rubber cast with pastel-coloured wax shot out through a little nozzle in the wax-melting machine in her bedroom. She stuck the wax rings branching out in all different directions on wax stalks. These miniature trees took hours, since you had to try many times to get the wax rings and pendants perfect – no missing grooves or air bubbles. The trees were then enclosed in a cylinder, and plaster would be poured into this cylinder and put in the kiln to set while the wax melted away, creating a mould for the rings. Gold would be poured into these plaster moulds and left to harden. When the plaster was washed away, what emerged were real little gold-ring trees. My mother would cut off the rings from the trunk one by one, as if she were pruning a bonsai tree.

These rings would be filed down, leaving no trace of where they had been connected to the trunk. Afterwards, the jewellery pieces would be hand-polished with a piece of jade. Clients mostly ordered 24-carat gold creations. Why anyone would want to wear pale metal mixtures was beyond the understanding of her Asian customers. The brighter, the better. Besides the usual orders for Buddha pendants, there were also huge pendants of Jesus with beads of pure gold blood dripping down his tormented face, BMW pendants and Mercedes Benz logos.

My mother would deliver her wares wrapped up in face-washers and dishcloths. She visited shops in Footscray, Richmond, Springvale and St Albans. She carried all her merchandise in her handbag, and that handbag was always close to her side. Sometimes customers would not pay up, or owe her gold and not give it back. She relied only on their promises, which were written on scraps of old paper or scrawled in her notebook in numerical form. There was no legal redress if she was gypped or cheated, since all she had to rely on was the good faith of her buyers. And the waiting! The waiting at the jewellery shops was the worst. Some of them were so small they did not have any chairs. Whenever a customer came in, the jewellery shop owner would serve that customer first, pushing aside the handful of gold nestled in crumpled paper napkins; ignoring the mother with the handful of kids breathing on the glass cabinets.

I could never wear gold myself. All those trays, all those hours of work, all those hours of leaving me to look after the babies when all I wanted to do was my own thing, until I no longer knew what my own thing was. My mother didn't wear gold either. "Some people walk around dripping with gold," she said, "showing how much they own, while their husbands are working in factories. Hmmph. I don't know why some men are so stupid. Anyway, if you are already beautiful, you don't need jewellery. And if you aren't, then there is not much a pair of dangly gold earrings can do, is there?"

My mother walked down the streets of Footscray as if she were a much larger, heavier person; with her legs apart in large thumping steps, the bones of her ankles creaking. She walked as if she were completely oblivious to her diminutive size. A person of such petite proportions was meant to be delicate, breakable, breathless. Yet my mother defied every law of her own physiology. Biologically she was destined to be delicate, to age into a thin, tiny woman. Yet the decades of work filled out her frame, widened her shoulders, gave her hands like cracked coal and the pounding walk like thunder.

She negotiated. She supplied, she marketed, she chased up creditors. She did all that without being able to speak English. Fortunately the small-business owners she dealt with rarely spoke English either. They probably asked their primary-school-aged kids to help them fill in their business registration forms. Yet my mother never saw herself as a businesswoman. Businesspeople were the representatives from Sony and Sharp who came to see my father at work to negotiate the supply of a new range of televisions. Not housewives with a handbag filled with gold wrapped in McDonald's napkins.

"**W**HY is she having so many children when she can't even look after her first two?" my grandmother would tut-tut with her tongue. "Look at them, skinny and brown as beef jerky and dressed like beggars, those kids." Aunt Que had decided that while my mother was ill, it would be a better arrangement for everyone if my grandmother moved in to live with her. Every time my grandmother came back to visit or to collect more of her belongings, she would comment on the shambles.

With my grandma gone, I started looking dishevelled. No red ribbons in my hair, no egg for breakfast every morning. No potty beside the bed. No one beside me at night to tell me stories, except my little brother, Alexander, who snored like a motorbike. But I had finally worked out how to turn myself on and off like a tap, regardless of any anxiety or agitation, so no more smelling like weed fertiliser.

Still, relatives would shake their heads in dismay. Even my friend's parents would see me with another sibling on my hip, and exclaim, "What? Another one?" They would look at me as if I were responsible.

My mother's pregnancies were the worst times for all of us. My sister Alison was a heavy heaving pregnancy that made Ma's belly and ankles swell up and nothing she swallowed would stay down. Morning sickness, afternoon sickness, evening sickness. Our bare feet sticky, we would run with buckets, usually too late. She would throw up all over the tiled floors of our living room, our bathroom, our kitchen. "Get the mop, Agheare," she would gag at me. When the mess was cleaned up, she would continue to work in the garage, well into the early hours of the morning while we were sleeping.

The heavy brown curtains in our living room were always drawn, but we never had any visitors anyway. That was the year when I learned to be alone, the year I realised how solitary we were. I rarely ventured outside anymore, not even into the backyard. Instead, I explored every nook and cranny of the house. Once, in the small cupboard under my grandmother's brown Buddha shrine, I found a plastic bag filled with what seemed like black fur. When I opened the bag to see what was inside, I was shocked to discover hair. Human hair. One very long braid, and two long ponytails. Warm and firm as live creatures, the hair was the brown-black-orange colour you can only get when the sun fades away the ebony. It was tied together with rubber bands that crumbled away when I tried to pull them higher up. I was fascinated. How old was this hair? Whose hair was it? Why had my grandmother kept this hair? I straightened out the strands and found new rubber bands to tie up the ponytails. I took the plait and put it at the nape of my neck, hanging the end over my shoulder. The things I could do with hair this long! I was thinking of the ways I could explain to my friends how my hair had grown overnight, when my brother came into the room looking for his grey matchbox truck.

"Hey Alexander, look at this."

"How'd you get that hair?" he asked, steering away from me.

"I found it. In here." I pointed to the cupboard.

"Whose is it?"

"I don't know."

"It might be some dead person's!"

"Don't be stupid. Why would Granny want to keep the hair of some dead person?"

But I put the hair away, retied the plastic bag and placed it back in the cupboard.

A few weeks later, my grandmother came back to collect the rest of her belongings from our house. As she knelt down by her Buddha shrine, I told her, "Ah Ma, there is hair in there." I didn't want to sound as alarmed as I felt.

"Where?" asked my grandmother.

"In there." I crawled in the cupboard and brought out the plastic bag. "Here."

My grandmother didn't tell me off for going through her personal things.

"Ah," she said, holding the hair in her hands, stroking it as I did, looking at it as I did. How strange, I thought, Granny is too old to want two ponytails dangling from the sides of her head, isn't she? But then again, she always wore lipstick when she went out, so there was no telling what new beauty trend might take her fancy.

"This hair is your Auntie Que's," my grandmother explained. "When she was little, she would grow her hair long. I would always braid it for her before school. And whenever she had her hair cut, I thought wah! Such a waste of beautiful hair. So I tied it up and kept it."

"When your Auntie Hy Que was born," my grandmother told me, "I was so happy. At last, a girl. Your grandfather could not understand why I was so happy. But of course he couldn't, he was the one who had howled and bellowed at me for wanting to swap my son for a girl. I called her Hy – happiness, and I kept her long hair every time I gave her a haircut."

*

She could never forget the two who had died back in Cambodia. Her first babies. Two girls who would be forever toddlers, neither of them living long enough even to make it into family photographs.

When she was giving birth to the first, my grandpa took a chair and sat outside the room. When he heard the wahwahwah sound of the child crying, his foot stopped tapping on the floor and he stood up. The midwife came out and told him it was a girl. A girl! He sat back down. He was inconsolable.

"Ah sister, what are you going to name this beautiful baby girl?" the midwife asked. My grandmother was exhausted, and yes – how stupid of her, yet how was she supposed to know that a decade later she would yearn and ache for a girl-child? – she was disappointed. "Ask my husband," she said to the midwife. She didn't even have a name ready, such was her hope and expectation that she would give her husband what his first wife couldn't. She lay there, waiting to see what her husband would name this girl. Finally, the midwife came back. "I know a pretty name," she told her. "How about Ah Bo?" Precious treasure.

It was then that she knew my grandfather couldn't even be bothered choosing a name for his daughter. He left the job to some lowly uneducated midwife, and she couldn't even come up with a very original name. But Treasure was such a wonder to my grandmother – her first baby. She found it hard to believe

74

that such a tiny thing could grow and become a person. When she held the baby in her arms, she knew that it did not matter that she was not a boy. She would be educated, and my grandmother would love her so much. Ah, she was so much prettier than the children of my grandpa's first wife.

When a baby turns a month old, we say that they are a year old because we count the time they spend inside the mother's stomach. But because she was not a boy, when my grandmother's beautiful Treasure was one month old there was no huge celebration with oranges and cakes and people bearing gifts of gold.

And then three months after she was born, she became sick. And before she could even say Mahmah she turned all tense and hard. It happened in less than a day and a night – and she was gone too soon. "Such a beautiful baby," sighed my grandmother. And those natural curls, little curls on a Chinese baby! That was unheard of! Only Westerners had those natural curls. So before she was laid in the ground, my grandmother took out her scissors and cut off one of the little curls.

"When someone dies, you don't say they died, like you do here," my grandmother told me. "You say things like that so easily here – he's dead, she's dead, they die. We say, they are passing through their bodies. Or their bodies have passed through. The body doesn't matter, it is the soul that is important. And Ah Bo had a beautiful soul, so clean, so bright. Now she was going to a place where there is no more darkness."

Less than a year later, my grandmother knew she was going to have another baby. So soon, people said to her, so soon, sister! She thought that Buddha was kind to her to send her another one. My grandpa thought that she was cursed just like his first wife. Two girls. She wondered whether this one looked like Ah Bo. She tried to search for Ah Bo in her face, but this child was so different. And again my grandfather sat outside, and again the midwife asked for a name. Again he did not give one. So the midwife made up a name for the baby: MeiHuay she was called, beautiful flower. Every second girl is named beautiful this-or-that plant or other. These uneducated Chinese Cambodian midwives were really not very inventive with names. But my grandmother didn't care. She had another girl.

And anyway, her baby's common name didn't matter because no one called her a beautiful flower. No, when she was born, she was quite large. She had such a round face, and so much hair. "Ay sister," Ah YuKeng would joke, "your baby was born with a hat on top of her head! Look at all that hair! Did you eat a lot of noodles when you were carrying the baby?"

"Noodles!" scoffed my grandfather. "If it were the noodles, I would have a boy by now."

With babies, for the first few weeks you cannot tell what they will look like – whether they will be lovely or hideous. But as they grow, and as the hair flattens on their head, you find out. And my grandmother found out that her new baby wasn't pretty, but she had a strong-featured face. She had a good jaw and twinkling black eyes like marbles. "Such sturdy legs! Ah, are you sure you had a girl?" joked that woman from across the road. "You know, she looks just like a little brother!" And so that's what she became – Ah Di – Little Brother. Everyone from then on called her Ah Di.

"What do you think you are doing, giving her such a name?" my grandfather berated her when he heard her calling Little Brother to come and have her porridge. He watched the child toddle over, her little brown legs stepping on the ground as if she were marching. "Such a strong and balanced child," my grandmother told him. "Look at how other babies wobble when they walk. They sway this way and that, and one little gust of wind would knock them flat. But look at your daughter, so balanced!"

"She's built like a boy," said my grandfather, "and now you've given her that terrible name. She's going to grow up like a boy if you're not careful, and then no one will want her. Who wants a girl always running about this way and that? Keep that child still, and stop calling her Little Brother! What do you think it is – some kind of joke? Do you think it's funny hah?"

But she could not help it. Little Brother stuck. And every time my grandfather came by, she stuck close to my grandmother.

"You've not given me a son, but a daughter who is like a son!" he said to my grandmother. "Woe, what could be worse?" Yet she didn't think that Little Brother was so much like a boy. She would try to teach her to be more graceful, but she was just a baby. A baby with balance. She still had Treasure's little dresses, and she put them on Little Brother, but Little Brother would always get them dirty. Put holes in them where no child could possibly make a hole. Also, she was a dribbler, and the front of her dresses would always be wet.

So what could my grandmother do? She sewed her many suits. And all in pretty colours, so no one could say that she was like a boy – pink, pale green and yellow. Especially red. "Aiya," neighbours would complain, "your daughter is so naughty, always climbing here and there! One day she is going to fall down and then it will be doom." That's why my grandmother

77

was so worried about Little Brother. "Aiyoh, Little Brother," she would yell, whenever she saw the girl climb up the metal stairs in the alleyway. "Little Brother! Come down now! No, you wait there! Don't move! I am coming!" She would grab her and take her inside. She would give her some smacks, of course, although smacking your child is like smacking your own flesh – it hurts. But she did not want anything bad to happen to Little Brother. She would make sure she stayed inside from now on. "Aiyoh, Little Brother," she would sigh, "why do you cause me such grief? Why do you always run off? Why are you always getting into danger? Why do you cause me such worry? Why can't you be a good kid?"

And Little Brother would be on the floor, howling and crying mahhhamagghhh sounds, filled with fury. Such anger! Such anger for such a little person. "Why are you so nasty for a little person?" my grandmother would say to her, and Little Brother would scream some more. "Let me out! Let me out to play!" She felt sad for Little Brother, but she had to learn not to be so naughty.

Yet, as Little Brother grew, she clung to my grandmother less and less, and soon stopped altogether, except when she was in a fury. Then she would pull at my gran's pants until her hands were all white. It was hard to shake her off. At other times, Little Brother loved to run and hide from my grandmother, and my grandmother saw everyone looking at her and making disdainful clicking noises with their tongues. "What a bad little girl," they would say. "What a messy little girl." And she was ashamed, she who was so neat.

"That woman doesn't know how to raise a daughter," she knew they were saying. "That woman doesn't know how to discipline her own child. But what do you expect from a younger second wife? She must be a bit loose herself, if you know what I mean."

"What a bad girl you are, Little Brother!" my grandmother said to her, fully aware of the sad irony of those words. Because if Little Brother really were a Little Brother, then she would still say the same words – "What a bad boy you are, Little Brother!" – but her sighs would be sighs of pride. Ah, look at my son, she would think to herself, so vibrant and active. So good. So good to be so vibrant and active. And the other women, those idle gossips, they would also say, "Ah, take a look at Huyen's son. Even though that woman was the second wife, she produced for her husband such a fine handsome boy. Look how active he is. Look how naughty he is, how cheeky! That boy is going to go far, he knows what he wants, eh? Look at him howling to go outside! He's going to be a traveller and cause you much grief, Huyen Thai!" they would joke. And she would laugh with them.

Oh, Little Brother, born in the year of the monkey! So cheeky, so cheery when she wanted to be. My grandmother would look at my grandfather's other children, the ones from The Other Side. Such bland faces, such dull creatures! And here was her Little Brother, cute as a puppy, so lovable, but not able to behave. Whenever my grandfather would come for a visit, my grandmother would have to neaten her up. Comb her hair, tie ribbons in it. Put on a pretty frock, Little Brother.

"No!"

"Look how beautiful this dress is!" she would coax.

"No!" Little Brother was such a stubborn one, standing there in the corner, her hands crossed over her chest.

Then my grandmother had to resort to bribes. "Put on this dress and I will buy you an ice lolly!"

"You're lying," she would yell. "Ma's always lying to me!"

Finally, she had to resort to threats: "Put on this dress or else you will be smacked!"

There was only one thing that scared Little Brother, and that was my grandfather. Whenever he came by, she would be quiet and well-behaved. So whenever my grandmother knew that my grandfather was visiting, she would have to prepare Little Brother. But sometimes he would come by unexpectedly, and he would catch her doing something wild. Chasing the chickens with holes in the knees of her pants. Sucking on an ice-lolly, an orange trail dribbling down her chin. Scratching marks on the wall with bits of black charcoal. "Discipline that child!"

At night my grandmother would sleep with her, curled up like one of those little grey beetles with the many legs – oh, how she loved that Little Brother. "Ma, Ma, tell me a story," Little Brother would beg. "Ma, can you tell me a story?"

"Too tired," my grandmother would mumble. "Too tired from you running around all day and causing trouble for me!"

"I'll be good!" she would promise. "I'll be good, Ma! Tell me a story!"

My grandmother sighed. "There was once a little girl who was always messy," she would begin. "The girl was always doing things to torment her mother ..." Oh, how Little Brother loved those stories, although she never learned from them. She just loved stories. Sometimes my grandmother would be too tired to invent a didactic tale, and it was at those times that she would just tell her the stories of Monkey. How Little Brother loved those myths! "You are such a little Monkey," my grandmother would tell her, "and when you are bad I should get a little gold band made for your head, eh?" She would giggle, that Little Brother wrapped up in her blanket like an insect in a cocoon. "Go to sleep now."

Soon my grandmother was pregnant again. Again, my grandfather hoped for a boy. Little Brother watched my grandmother's stomach bloat round like a ball and heard everyone's hopes and expectations: "Must be a boy, look how big the tummy is!" "Wouldn't it be good if it was a boy!" And my grandmother would tell the little girl, "Ah, Little Brother, wouldn't it be good if you had a little brother?"

The child didn't understand. "But *I am* Little Brother," she would say.

This time, my grandmother was lucky. My eldest uncle was born. After his birth, my grandfather returned to live with my grandmother. "Oh, how clever Huyen Thai is!" the women in the neighbourhood would say. "To have such a beautiful big baby boy, and her husband back!" Stupid city women with countryside intellects! She knew it had nothing to do with being clever or not clever.

Of course, when the new baby was a month old, my grandfather wanted the whole town to know that he had had a boy at last, after so many years. So he planned for a big celebration and invited many people. My grandmother was excited too, because she knew everyone would see how much he loved her, and how she was the superior wife. So the day was set, and food was ordered. Five roast ducks, crackling pork, so many oranges and, of course, the lucky red candy. All day my grandfather would hold the baby boy – he did not, of course, pay any attention to Little Brother. And my grandmother was so busy with preparing the big feast that she got annoyed with Little Brother, who was pulling at her pants-legs and asking her all sorts of questions: "Why are you making all this food?" "Who is coming over?" "Why are all these people coming over?"

Finally, my grandmother snapped, "Children shouldn't be so nosey! Go away and play by yourself, Little Brother!" In the end, she handed the little girl a lolly on a stick, the kind that you can suck for an hour and not cause any trouble for the adults. "Now go and play." And it was only then that Little Brother let go of her trouser leg and waddled off.

About half an hour later, my grandmother heard my grand-father yell, "No! These are for your brother's guests! What a greedy thing, you have one already!"

"But he can't even eat them and he has a whole bowl!" she heard Little Brother sulk, and then she knew she was trying to get at the lollies on the table.

"What a rude little girl!" my grandmother heard my grand-father bellow, and then Little Brother screaming and yelling and howling. She was throwing one of her tantrums, and my grandmother had no time for her tantrums.

"Little Brother," my grandmother said as she entered the guest room. "Stop that! Stop that or else I will smack you!"

But she wouldn't stop. "Pa took away the lollies!" she screamed, "Pa took away the lollies!" Her own lollypop had popped out of her mouth and was lying in a wet puddle on the ground.

"Aiyaah," my grandmother moaned, picking up the lolly-stick and realising that it had stained the floor red, "what trouble you are! Stop crying!"

She looked around and could see that my grandfather had

placed the tray of lollies on the very top shelf. She grabbed one and gave it to Little Brother. Little Brother whacked it out of her hands, not wanting it. She began squealing on the floor. From the other room, my grandfather bellowed, "Shut that child up! Her little brother is trying to sleep!"

"I am not trying to sleep!" Little Brother screamed. "I don't want to sleep! I want more than just one lolly! Why does that baby get the whole tray?" She would not stop screaming and kicking and howling.

"Little Brother, be quiet or else your father will give you a thrashing!" my grandmother warned, but it was no use. She decided that the best thing to do was to ignore her and go back to preparing the food. She prayed that her father would not come and belt her for making such noise, but if he did, she deserved it.

She could hear my grandfather coming in to the guest room. "What do you think you are doing?" he said to Little Brother. "How can a child be so greedy?"

And Little Brother tried to quieten down. She was trying so hard!

He yelled, "Can't you see that your little brother is sleeping?"

And her sobbing quietened even more.

My grandmother rushed into the guest room. "Don't hit her," she told your grandfather. "She really has stopped. Those hic-hic sounds – every child makes them when they have cried for too long. They can't help making those noises."

After my grandfather left the room, my grandmother said to Little Brother sternly, "Now, no more of that sooking, you hear me? Be good, and I will give you an ice lolly tonight." My grandmother handed her back her lollypop, washed, and also the lolly she had thrown away. "Here," my grandmother said, "now you have two lollies, and you will get some more tonight if you are good." She watched Little Brother put the lollypop in her mouth and, now satisfied, went back into the kitchen to cut up the huge slab of roast pork with the big meat cleaver.

My grandmother probably often thought back to the what-ifs. What if she had done things differently, would the bad thing that happened still have happened? Why is it that when her luck was good, something bad had to happen, something that she could never have expected? And she probably also often thought, all those years of not having another girl – the gods were probably punishing her for what happened to Little Brother. For not being careful. She should have taken her into the kitchen with her. Oh, but the meat cleaver was so sharp, and she was such a distracting girl, pulling at this and that! And the kitchen was tiny, much smaller than the one in our house in Braybrook! Of course much smaller than that. She thought that Little Brother would be good in the guest room, sucking on her lollies.

She should not have cut up the pork then. Oh, why did she have to cut up the pork? Why couldn't she have done a quieter chore, like washing the vegetables or even moulding the agar-agar? Because, as her cleaver went up and down and bam and bom, she was thinking about how terrible Little Brother's tantrums were. Oh, why did she need to be so spoilt? Why did the gods give her a girl with the temperament of a boy? Bom bom went her cleaver, and bom bom went her thoughts. Why couldn't Little Brother have been a boy? Then she would have a happier life! Bom Bom. That is why my grandmother did not hear what Little Brother was up to until the final BOM! that did not come from her cleaver. It came from the guest room.

My grandfather was there before her, and so was their servant. But the first thing she noticed when she ran into the room was that the top shelf of their set of shelves had fallen, and was lying, split in the middle, on the floor. My grandmother looked at the floor and saw the lucky lollies scattered everywhere – red drops all over the floor. The servant was screaming and wailing, "Aiyaah! What has happened? How could this have happened? Why?" And my grandfather was yelling at her, "Shut up, you stupid woman, stop the screaming! You are making it worse for my wife!" Then he turned to my grandmother: "I told you not to give her those lollies on a stick! How many times have I told you that, and still you don't listen to me!"

I remember a cautionary tale my grandmother told me when I was little, about how I was never to run around with pencils or pens in my mouth. When she was young, in my grandmother's street there was a child who died because he fell from his chair with a chopstick in his mouth. It poked right through to the back of his head.

"Let me see Little Brother!" my grandmother screamed, and this time my grandfather did not tell her, "How many times have I told you to stop calling the child that?" He and the servant would not let her see her own child. Her own blood and flesh! She screamed and screamed, she screamed until the other little brother in the other room woke up, she screamed until there was nothing my grandpa or the servant could do but step aside and let her hold her baby with the matted hair like a little hat.

WHEN I was nine, I made a whole clan of forty-two tiny dolls, boys included, with hand-stitched woollen hair. I even embroidered each of their faces. I made twins and triplets, a community of mermaids and some villains. I brought them to school in a white plastic bag, and Beatrice and I played with them during our lunchtimes. The dolls made us forget about the stigmas of our physical selves – the nits and grotty fingernails, my capital P Perm and Beatrice's nest of red hair. Beatrice was an infinitely better person than I, she forgave easily. We made the dolls into the people we would have liked to be, killed the ones we deemed unfit to live, and made up elaborate tales of love and deceit to rival those of the screenwriters of *Neighbours*. We reigned in our world, and I felt supreme. I was the creator. "Did you make any more?" Beatrice would ask me each morning, and I would show her.

At home I would put the little dolls away and pick up the howling baby.

"*Wheeen* are you going to be done?" I whinged.

"Half an hour, just half an hour," coaxed my mother. Or, "Forty minutes, just forty minutes." The kiln was fired up, she was ready to do work. The whole garage was whirring and throbbing and there was no stopping her. "But that's what you always say and then you go for hours and hours," I whined, and

I could already feel my arms aching. I learned to prepare baby formula, to squirt the bottle onto my wrist to test whether it was too hot. I learned to feed my baby sister Alison who would suck for six seconds and then push the bottle out of her mouth with her tongue. I would then have to distract her, so that she would forget that she didn't want to drink.

Half an hour became one hour, one hour became two, and my mother would be done and pick up the baby for a little while, and then say that she had to head off to do deliveries. I was to look after the sister well or else – if anything should happen, by God, I would be doomed. I had no time left to do anything. Then when I had time to do anything I would sit around fuming over how long it took for there to be time to do anything, and there would be nothing much for me to do because you never knew when the baby was going to start howling again. And I fumed because Ma never told me what a good sister I was and how much I loved the baby, just kept warning me not to do evil to her, not to take my eyes off her, not to let her roll off the bed, because "You know how babies roll themselves off the bed, even ones that can't crawl yet."

And then one day she did.

There was a loud bang from the bedroom where I had left her on the bed, lying on her tummy with her head sticking up. When I ran back into the room again my sister was on the floor, howling and flailing her arms and legs in the air like a red beetle turned on its back.

"What happened?" my mother yelled, rushing into the room.

"Alison kicked herself off the bed!"

She grabbed the baby from the floor and yelled, "I told you

to look after your sister and I turn my back just one minute and there she is on the floor howling! Wretched woe, who knows what may happen to her now! Haven't I always warned you that babies have very soft thin skulls? They are born with a hole in their heads before their skulls close up and if they fall they become retarded! Did she fall on her head? How did she fall? HOW DID SHE FALL?"

"I don't know."

"You don't know! You don't know! You don't know because you weren't looking after her, were you? I don't know what use you are, with nothing better to do with your time! You can't even look after your sister for just one second without her falling off the bed to her death. If she is brain-damaged, then you are doomed! Woe, aiyyooo, I'm going to call your father right now, so he can take her to the hospital to have her head examined. Such is the woe of my life to have a child who is always bumming around doing no good! You wait, you just wait."

So I waited. I waited with my hands tearing little anxious holes in my pockets while my mother rushed off to light some incense. She handed me a stick and then knelt on the floor, frantically shaking the stick back and forth. "Buddha, bless little Alison and keep her safe even though her sister wasn't looking after her properly and she fell off the bed. Buddha, bless the safety of our little one and keep her safe from harm and evil." At this point my mother gave me a long hard look.

I wondered whether anyone Up There would be convinced by my newfound piety, but I tried anyway. If my sister was okay, I prayed, I would do all my jobs without complaining. I would commit my soul to servitude forever and ever. I would be as uncomplaining as an automaton, I would not whinge whenever

I heard "half an hour more", I would learn to be just a speck and do things for the greater good of the family.

Then I realised that if Buddha did exist, if God did exist, if any deity Up There did exist, then why the hell was He tormenting me so with my sister falling off the bed right at the very moment when I was merely getting a new book to read? Probably just as I suspected, His plan for me was not to learn at all, but to be forever in a state of staying at home and looking after babies and cleaning up crap and not being able to rid myself of the smell and the dirt. It was time for me to learn some acceptance.

Dear Lord, I will not defy this fate you have for me if you make my sister alright. I will not even question Your plan. Just let my sister be alright and You can even turn me into a worm in my next life.

While I was renouncing all my doubts to The One Up There, my father came home. "What happened?" he demanded.

"She fell off the bed," I repeated, wondering if adults were really such amnesiacs, because only twenty minutes ago I had heard my mother on the phone yelling, "Wretched woe, aiya-aaahhhh, Agheare wasn't looking and Alison was kicking and she kicked herself off the bed! Come quick, come quick!"

"Can't even be responsible for anything, not even looking after your own sister for a little while," my father tut-tutted with his tongue. It was not the time to tell him that the "little while" had been hours and hours.

Ma and Pa bundled my screaming sister into the car and drove off, leaving me standing in the doorway wiping my nose with my sleeve. If my sister was brain-damaged it would be my fault – after today all the cuteness would be erased from her face and she would be a drooling drone. And everywhere I went people would point and say, "Ah, look, there's that girl who made her sister retarded because when she was nine she couldn't even mind her for a few moments!"

I decided that if my sister came back from the hospital brain-damaged, my life was indeed doomed. I then decided quite rationally that since there was nothing to live for, I might as well doom myself before my parents came home and did the job themselves. Yet how to doom oneself painlessly?

In the Chinese serials my grandmother loved to watch, whenever some noble warrior wanted to end it all, he drew out his sword and impaled himself. Then he would lie there, spluttering all sorts of regrets while his beloved comrades cradled his head and wailed. A slow, neat rivulet of blood would trickle from his mouth.

I hated blood. Too often had I seen my mother accidentally stab her hand with the scalpel she used to cut open the wax moulds, or chop her finger with our butcher's cleaver, to think that the traditional Chinese death by a thousand cuts was something noble.

I thought about hanging, which wasn't such a bad idea if I wasn't so small and therefore unable to reach anything high enough to be a beam. Then I recalled that the monkey bars at Tottenham North Primary School were pretty high because when I swung from them, my feet were a long way from the ground.

I could bring a scarf.

But then I thought of my body dangling there overnight, and how the Totty Tech boys might arrive in the morning and think it hilarious to pull down my pants.

Suddenly I remembered reading something about plants in the *Reader's Digest Household Hints and Handy Tips*, a thick black volume which my father had bought for me one summer. I remembered reading about the Oleander bush, which we had in our backyard, with its bright pink flowers that looked like tissue paper. "Those flowers are poisonous," my father would tell us. "Always wash your hands if you have accidentally touched them." I read case studies of children who had eaten the flowers and died. Flowers were a good way to end it all, I thought. I looked out of our kitchen window to make sure that the bush was in bloom. It was, in all its pink-tissue-paper glory. I decided to go to bed and wait for my parents to call and give me the sign as to whether I should go outside and meet my Maker through the Oleander plant portal.

I closed my eyes. Sudden snatches of imagined conversation – "funny-shaped head now, like a potato, and what is wrong with her *eyes*?"; remembered precepts – "take care of her"; coiled-up whimpers and anticipated cries of fury all ricocheted about my mind. My stomach seemed to be hollow. I curled up in foetal position, I spread myself flat in corpse pose, I squelched my face on the pillow as if struck from the back. No rest for the wicked, I thought. I fell into an exhausted black sleep.

"You are lucky," said my mother, when she returned.

My father nodded. "You are very lucky there is nothing wrong with her."

The little bundle was in my hands again and I was squeezing the tiny snot-nosed sook so tightly and feeling such a sense of love and relief that I forgot I was also meant to be exuberant that I did not need to doom myself.

"**Y**OU must be an example to your younger siblings," my parents told me. "You see, Agheare," my father explained, "a family is like a snake. If the head of the snake is set straight, then the rest of the body follows straight. However, if the head is crooked, then the body gets as bent as ginseng and it is doomed." How to keep my head on, let alone straight? I wished that I was born meek and good, instead of dissatisfied and resentful. How could I fill my time usefully instead of always bumming around reading books?

There was one form of work that alleviated some of the guilt – sewing. I made berets from the fleecy factory scraps that my Third Auntie Samso brought home for our family to use as floor wipes. I created stuffed animals, dogs with floppy ears and button eyes. I learned embroidery from library books, fabricated patchwork cushions and designed clothes for my sisters Alison and Alina. People always assumed that the digital dexterity of Asians was a genetic trait, some God-given talent. But that was not entirely true. While other kids were glueing icy-pole sticks onto paper plates, Asian kids were attaching eye-hooks to designer skirts because their parents' eyesight was failing.

Neither of my parents could sew, but before I started high school they saved and saved to present me with my first love.

His name was Janome. He had a beautiful cream-coloured complexion, and all the pieces of my life began to fit together after I met him. He worked wonders with me. We functioned as a unit, so completely in synch with each other's movements that it was magical. Sewing was essentially like driving a car. You pushed your foot on the pedal, and guided by the light of the machine, you made the lines swerve and twist and turn towards some distant point far from home.

I started off with children's clothes. The comparative shapelessness of their little bodies meant that fitting was easy – no complicated tucks and darts. I bought patterns and taught myself how to piece them together. I made myself a party frock in blue taffeta, complete with hundreds of hand-sewn sequins and an invisible zip. Clothes that were bought on sale didn't necessarily match with other items bought on sale. Sometimes they didn't fit properly, but we were left to grow into them. I doubted that our arms would grow down past our calves, or our shoulders to our elbows. But now with my beloved Janome, I worked miracles.

And self-made miracles were exactly what sustained me through my adolescent years, when other girls were getting into trendy clothing labels and boys. Pretending that I had nothing more to worry about than which new Sportsgirl summer dress I should purchase was already too much trouble – especially when I had to hand-embroider the accursed Sportsgirl logo, with all its curves and flourishes, onto my self-designed creations. Who needed to smoke ciggies or get petted by boys or drink booze when I was already a rebel of the most exciting kind? I was a veritable *pirate*.

Because I seemed to have nothing better to do with my

time than practise for an outworking career, relatives would leave their children with me when they went out, or whenever they had "other things to do". "Ah, Agheare is so good, she is so responsible," they would say. "We can always trust her with our children and they won't get hurt."

"Why don't they make Alexander do it?" I would complain to my mother.

"He doesn't know how to look after babies. He's a boy. Besides you are more responsible and mature than he is."

I was not won over by their sedulous flattery. Girls only matured faster because they had to do more. I hated housework, and I often let my mother know it in no uncertain terms. "I am so busy, and you do this to me!" my mother would scream, almost in tears, "working till I am so tired, and none of you ever help out, and your father is always saying, wah, don't let them work, they have to study, while I have to do everything and still you are so bad and do this to me! Aiiyyyaaaahhh, why do you do this to me?!" And then I would feel infinitely guilty. What to do, I thought, when one was responsible for the torment of the family and in grave danger of becoming a lady?

A lady was the most abhorred thing you could become, because ladies were lazy bums who sat around wasting their husband's money and walked down the street with perfectly made-up mien visiting the jewellery stores to which my mother delivered her wares. My mother was certainly not a lady. She worked and worked and worked, and when she wasn't working she was cleaning, and when she wasn't cleaning or working she was sick. You could always tell who was a lady by what they complained about, the length of their nails and whether they put milk or butter into their coffee.

94

Instant coffee was my panacea in these years. I put International Roast powder into everything, even our milder forms of Chinese herbal medicine like Lou Han Guo and Chrysanthemum Tea. I would drink cupful after cupful mixed with sweetened condensed milk. It gave me the shakes, but I didn't care. Sometimes the milk would run out, and I would have to improvise by using coconut milk. Sometimes we would not have any sugar left, and I would use jam. I would also throw in a few spoonfuls of Milo.

"Consider yourself lucky," my mother scolded me. "When I was young, we couldn't just walk to the kitchen whenever we felt the fancy to have a drink, and make ourselves a cup of coffee with Sweet and Condensed Milk. We had to work; we never had a mother at home to take care of us. We had one doll, shared among the eight of us, and I went out to earn my own way when I was thirteen."

For me there was housework, and then there was homework to alleviate the boredom of the housework. And then there were books. When I was thirteen, I devoured *Dolly* fiction the way stuck-at-home housewives devoured Fabio romances. The only Asian girls in those romances were named Momoko or Ginny and came from educated middle-class families. How I hated the clean-cut beauty of these characters, who were having a grand old time without worrying about their poor mothers working their fingers to the bone; without feeling guilty because there wouldn't be anyone to watch over the screaming sibling, or wipe the floors or clean the house or hang out nappies.

Coming of Age was explained to me in books, and in the books Judy Blume characters waited with delirious anticipation for their period. I didn't see what the big deal was when it happened to me. So what? It just meant I could make babies if I felt the urge, and of course that was the last thing on my mind. So I wrote the date in my diary, and dreary life continued on as usual. Coming of Age for boys was infinitely more interesting, I thought, when I watched *Stand by Me* and *Dead Poets Society*. Boys formed friendships by discovering cadavers. They walked on railway tracks, started secret clubs, cried over their own cowardice and occasionally shot themselves in the head when pushed too far. It didn't matter if girls were cowards, there was no opportunity or reason for us to test our bravery. All that mattered was that we could make a good pot of rice, had a pretty face and were fertile.

A few years later, my Auntie Bek, my mother's eldest sister, asked me, "Eh, Agheare, did your mother have a big celebration for you when your time came?"

"Huh?"

"You know, with lots of food, and a new set of clothes in red, and lots of rejoicing?"

"No."

"Why didn't you celebrate Agheare's coming of age?" my auntie asked my mother.

"Hah?" said my mother, "don't be ridiculous, no one does that anymore."

Girls came of age so easily, all they had to do was start bleeding and they were certified women, which meant that they had to be kept mostly at home because of all the rapists out there. "You never know," my father would say shaking his head, "what kind of people are out there."

"You never know," said my mother, "how dirty-minded men are."

My parents painted a picture of a world in which every man under the age of twenty was a precocious pervert and every man over twenty a potential paedophile.

But the boys in the *Dolly* romances I read were never the phantom types that walked around with permanent bulges looking for nubile Lolitas. They were always sweet lads named Laurie or Jesse or Bradley. They smiled a lot and said things like, "Oh Linn, I never realised what nice almond eyes you have," and they let their girl rest her head on their shoulder without fear of catching lice.

Yet I knew no Laurie or Jesse or Bradley would tell me, "Hey Alice you are lovely," because I wasn't, or "Hey Alice you're sweet," because I probably smelt like Johnson's baby piss, or "Hey Alice, will you be mine?" because I belonged to the house and the babies and they would never discover me inside the concrete walls of Number 3, Bliss Street, Braybrook. I imagined myself wasting away like a princess in a tower, or rather a caffeine addict in a shack behind the Invicta carpet factory.

None of the boys in my neighbourhood would qualify as Bradley or Laurie, because Bradley or Laurie did not smash empty glass bottles on the road for fun and terrorise the local senior citizens. Bradley and Laurie were usually blue-eyed, blonde-haired, they were never ever blue-haired, blonde-eyed. No, I was sure Brad did not laugh hysterically, screaming F-ing this and that.

I turned up the radio to drown out the boys outside, who were obsessed with fornicating perdition because they were yelling it at the top of their lungs. Then Mariah Carey came on the radio and sang "Dream Lover, come rescue me," so I turned off the radio. If by some miracle Dream Lover wanted to bother with that scrawny girl in the concrete house behind the Invicta carpet factory, Dream Lover would have to overcome several obstacles, including surviving the carpet fumes, getting past the broken glass on the road and avoiding getting a bottle pushed in his face. He would then have to find the house number, because my grandmother had written PUSH on the letterbox instead of Number 3, because my father had written PUSH on the garage door and she thought that was the name of our house.

And if Dream Lover wasn't a complete idiot standing there PUSHing the letterbox off its hinges, he would walk to the front door and ring the doorbell and pose himself in all manner of chivalry, and the door would open to reveal the darling exploited Proletarian Princess carrying the third-world gene.

"Who is that? Is that Brianna?" the ma of the Proletarian Princess is heard yelling from inside the house. "Tell her she can't come over, why is she always coming over?"

"No Ma, it's not Brianna," the Proletarian Princess mutters, staring through the iron-lace grating of the security door.

"Then who is it?"

"It's a ... another friend."

"Tell them to go away, tell them you have work to do! Shut the door! You're letting the factory fumes in. Get back inside! You haven't even wiped the floors properly! If I slip carrying this baby in my stomach, by God you are doomed. Always half-finishing things off, like a cat with a head and no tail." And so the door closes, and the Proletarian Princess walks sadly back into the house, realising that there are no Proletarian Princesses anyway and how could she possibly have been so thick as to imagine that Dream Lover would come rescue her from here in the first place?

*A*LL you want at fifteen is to have a boyfriend, not to choose the future father of your children. All a fifteen-year-old boy wants is to receive affirmation from a girl, and perhaps something more if he is lucky – not to choose the future daughter-in-law for his mother. All we wanted was someone to go to the movies with, to talk to when tormented by adolescent angst, and to show off to our friends.

"At this age, you must not get into relationships, you must study hard, your future is so important," my father told me. My father had grand images of me freshly processed from the tertiary production line and packed into a sterile office somewhere in Springvale, doing Very Important Work. It was all well and good to scream and cry for pretty dresses and plastic bonbons in the hair as a child, but when you reached adolescence, yearning for those very same things could spell doom. No longer is the little flaunter smiled upon, for to be a flaunter is the worst thing a girl can be. Button up your coat and don't think about such things. Boxed into your blue blazer, you sit at your desk and study, and that will settle you down. Back in the old country, the good girls stayed at home and the bad girls went out with baskets of oranges and apples late at night and made their money selling all sorts of fruit in the park.

Here it was different. The difference between our sweet

apple-smelling schoolgirl in Melbourne Central Station and our sweet apple-selling streetgirl in Central Market Phnom Penh was that one believed in free love, and the other did not. Australian democracy seemed to be available to all by the mere shedding of your clothes. Perhaps clothes did not even have to be discarded, because in broad daylight we would see the schoolgirls and boys in their school uniforms, full blazers and ties and kilts and long socks, lying atop each other in the park. There was no other place to go to lose themselves because their parents must not know, because their parents knew nothing about being free to love. Parents just didn't get it. Life was not to be spent at the mercy of sunken-faced migrants, bringing from the old country a million scruples that made no sense. Australians all let us rejoice, for we are young and free, not held tight in the clutches of the village gossip or the narrow-eyed matchmaker.

I was the cover-up girl for my friends, the one who watched and lived vicariously and answered the phone to let the parents know that Melissa was at my house even though I knew she was probably clambering in the window of Tung's room, dressed like a soft brown sausage poured into a tube of black vinyl, eyes lined with kohl. I was the one friends begged for evidentiary aid when the age-old excuses were all used up: "We have to go to the library." "We have to use the school's computer labs." "We have to meet up with friends for a group project."

Names were changed, new identities forged. "Oh, hello, Brianna," I would say into the phone when it was actually Bryan, and if the boy was too dumb to catch on, I hung up and called the real Brianna to lament.

*

"Who was that boy who rang before?" my mother demanded. She knew it was a boy because she had picked up and answered. "'Allo? 'Allo? You want Asunder?" She handed the phone to my twelve-year-old brother.

"Hello?" Alexander paused. He looked at me. Uh-oh. I glared at him and willed him to hang up.

"Errr, yes. She's here." Then, without thinking, he handed the phone over to me. "Here, it's for you."

"Hello?" I asked into the receiver, my voice squeaking. "Who is this?" "Just Alexander's friend," I lied after I hung up, wondering why I had to lie.

"How do you know him? He sounds too old to be your brother's friend." The questions were hurled at me like the pits of sour plums. "Why does he have our number?" "What did he want?" "Oh, so you spoke for *that* long about homework hah?"

How could I explain to my mother that we were just chatting, let alone what we were chatting about, when I did not have that many Teochew words in my head, and when the meaning of "chat" did not register in her mind? Boys did not talk to girls for no reason. "Boys should not talk too much," she said to me slowly. "Boys who have too many words are no good." She took a long look at me and I knew that the news was going straight to my father. Why did the words matter so much, anyway? "People talk," said my mother. "Boys talk to you, you talk to boys, and people talk."

Who were these people, and what did they talk about? How was it that they could see me but I could not see them? "They are walking together," people said. "I saw your daughter walking with a boy. I wonder who the boy is hah?" Even if the boy was walking two metres behind, even if he were a platonic friend, even if he were the loser from the Ha Thinh grocery store who followed me back to Retravision every afternoon after school, I would feel as though I was doing something wrong, and feel the inevitable guilt. Then he would feel the guilt, and we would both wonder what was going on, and whether it was true that he did like me in *that* way or whether I did like him in that way even though I was completely sure that I didn't, but perhaps my actions meant otherwise? Once I started acting awkward around somebody, they probably thought that I liked them, and once both people started acting awkward, it meant that the parents could come and stand over us and call us "Ah Di" and "Ah Mui", Little Brother and Little Sister, and make sure we'd never want to be within a seven-kilometre radius of each other again.

*

"Your parents think you went out with Vincent on Sunday." Cousin Andrew had called me on the phone to tell me what I already knew. I thought, this is all his mother's doing, this is all my mother's doing. "You know I didn't, and that's none of your business anyway," I sighed.

"It is when your parents come over to my house and start asking me questions!"

My parents had come over to his house to interrogate him!

"So what happened?" Andrew asked.

"Nothing. He called me and my mother answered and made a few crazy connections in her mind. And now I am stuck here all holidays. Can't go anywhere in case they think I'm going out with boys and getting corrupted."

"This is stupid. Why don't you tell them that nothing has happened?"

"I did. I can't."

After two weeks of house arrest I was going crazy, with a barricade of books around my bed and the bedroom door closed from prying parents. But I had no need to fear for my inalienable right to privacy, because they knew I was not going anywhere, not going out with the Lee and Lah loiterers in any case. This was my mother's term for the boys who squatted on the benches in the park, wasting time.

What was most damning were not the things that were said, but the things left unsaid. And since there were so many things that I could not say, I exercised my right to remain silent until my silence was construed as guilt, and the guilt ensured my house arrest.

Nothing I said could protect me because it was automatically assumed that I could not protect myself. "But I didn't go out with anyone!" I would cry, and that cry would be taken as a sign of the frailty of youth, hypersensitive, hysterical – how could the elders ever think of trusting such a baby to her own devices if she got emotional over such little things so easily? Teary denials were the first sign of wrongdoing. "The worst thing that can happen to a girl is if she is tricked," my mother warned me. "There is no redemption for one who is tricked."

The most reasonable thing to do was to do the unreasonable, give people real cause to talk. The easiest solution would be to just call up the boy, ask him out even if I didn't like him in that way, and board a bus out of Braybrook. After all, it was only a five-minute walk to the bus stop. But I was paralysed. At the rate things were going, I thought, dating would be conducted under house arrest too, if the elders had anything to do with it. Watching from afar and making up complicated stories about uncomplicated young people was bad enough. Worse still would be to bring a potential partner home to be watched. I could just imagine it. We would be sitting opposite each other at the table doing homework while my mother cut up spring onions on the kitchen bench. The best we could do would be to pass notes to each other like school-children watched over by the headmistress.

"You know, good young men are not sneaky and they respect parents," my father told me, standing in the doorway of my bedroom. But fifteen-year-olds were boys, not young men; there were many things they did not know. My brother did not know. Vincent did not know. Cousin Andrew did not know. Then how was it that I knew perfectly well the guilt and the agony and anticipated it in advance? From where did I learn this guilt-laden look over the shoulder?

During my two weeks of torment, I doubted the boy had any idea about the effect of his careless phone call, that it would annihilate all the days of my term break and leave me skulking in my room. "Your father can't even take you out to work at the shop," complained my mother "what with that expression on your face looking as if you were freshly dug out of the morgue!"

To raise a girl, I realised, you'd need gallons of Social Conditioner with added Spirit Deflator. Rub onto every limb until limp, put the child into a chair and wait until she sets. When appendages harden, you know you have a perfect young woman – so still and silent and sedate that you could wrap your precious one up in cotton wool and put her in a cabinet. Ah, look at the darling geisha behind glass.

*

"Love sensibly," was my grandmother's advice to me before she died.

Yet she of all people would have realised that passion cannot be experienced sensibly – and it was her impassioned fight for peasant rights that had landed her in trouble in China when she was young. Her impoverished family had sent their daughter to get an education at Chaozhou Women Teacher's College, and after learning about Marx and the revolution of the masses she wrote articles for newspapers about land rights and landlord abuses. She really was the princess of the proletariat, and because they had no money, her currency was words, the exchange rate measured in truth.

But too much truth can land one in deep trouble, especially if those in power only like the *idea* of the starving peasants. The idea was good political ammunition, but the reality was something else altogether. These peasants were the disenfranchised and disempowered in China, wrote my grandmother, the valuable but suffering *real* people. Help us, she wrote. Help. Us.

Get lost, they told her, get lost or we will get you.

So I imagine my grandmother Huyen Thai as a young woman arriving in Cambodia with her brother. It is a familiar story – the revolutionary fleeing a homeland that is now hunting her down. She would never see her beloved Long Mountain again. She would never again see her home village, her parents or the women teachers' college for which they sacrificed so much to send her to. What she saw now was the heat, the colour and the crowd of a strange city with a stranger name. The revolution, it appeared, was only just beginning and now she was so far away from it all, she could not participate in it, she could not see it, she could not even write about it. So she found herself a job as a schoolteacher at the DongHua Chinese school. It was there that she met my grandfather.

Who would have thought that the old teacher and the young girl fresh off the boat from Long Mountain would become such kindred spirits? Who would have thought that they would share a mindset? But they did. My grandfather must have thought that there was something extraordinary about the young woman who drew chalk circles on the concrete and made children stand in them instead of using the ruler for discipline like everyone else. And my grandmother must have seen something in my grandfather, the unsmiling solemn man with a Mao Ze Dong mole on his chin. She must have been assailed by some strange disease, some affliction that women of my family continued to speak about behind her back, even after her death. When they spoke of it, it was always in hushed, incredulous tones – that someone who had made rational decisions all her life would go a bit ding-dong and decide to pursue a man more than ten years her senior who already had a wife and children. It was a revelation that brought secret consolation to legions of suffering daughters-in-law. "Did you know that your grandmother had to carry tea to your grandfather's first wife?"

Diseased with love, they called it, those who watched like hawks to note any departure from sense. They said things like, "Woe and wah, she is diseased with him very deeply," as if the

107

two people were rotted by love, and already melding into one contagious sticky miasma. It was a terminal illness.

*

Deep in my emotional quagmire, I was sitting hunched over my desk. I had been like this for more than a week, a listless sad-sack, feet tucked under the chair and head whammy on the tabletop, quivering like agar-agar. I heard the doorbell ring, but I refused to move. I could hear my mother's thumping footsteps at the front door, and the squeal of the hinges of the iron-lace security door. "Aiyah! Sister! How good to see you!" she exclaimed, and I knew it was not one of her own sisters come to visit. "Come in! Come in! Sit down! Sit down!" Fragments of conversation drifted in to me, but I was too tired to notice. I would be glad when all this was over, I thought, when I could get back to school again and immerse myself in home-work. I would be glad when I did not need to think about whether the next phone call would induce a new round of inter-rogation. Dressed in old tracksuit pants and a holey brown jumper, my socks pulled over my pants up to my knees, I was too embarrassed to go out to face anybody.

Suddenly, a rotund woman appeared in the doorway of our room. I wanted to acknowledge her only by blinking. Any other movement took too much energy. Funny, but people looked small sideways. In fact, I could make her disappear entirely by squeezing my eyes into smaller and smaller slits. My mother was standing behind her. "This is my daughter," she said to the woman. Then she turned to me. "Agheare," she said, "this is Auntie Ah BuKien."

"Wah! So grown-up now!" the woman exclaimed. I managed

to lift my head up off the table, pretending that too much study had made my brain heavy.

"Do you remember me?" I hadn't the faintest clue who she was, and didn't know whether to lie or tell the truth, so I smiled, because I knew that a smile was always the right answer for a girl.

"I knew you when you were little, and look at you now!" she exclaimed.

And look she did. In fact, she was *really* watching me. She didn't see the ugliness, she didn't see the lack of energy, she didn't see the deflated spirit, and of course she refused to see that I had been stuck at home for two weeks sedated by a handful of *Reader's Digest*s and dreary *Dolly* fiction. What she saw was a quiet little seated saint.

"Agheare is so good, she stays at home and studies," said Ah BuKien, "and wah, she has such a pretty little nose."

*M*Y mother and father still call each other "old man" and "old woman". My mother got her title first. When she was thirteen, one day she was waiting at the corner of the street in Phnom Penh with all the other little factory girls for the rain to stop so they could walk home. My father felt sorry for them and picked them all up in his factory van. As she got in the van, my mother almost slipped on the first step because of her wet shoe soles. "Watch your step eh, old lady," my father said, steadying her.

"I never thought I would end up with your father," my mother told me. "I can still remember the day of his engagement, because that day I was working at the factory. I don't think he remembered me much, because I was just a little kid." She was only thirteen then, and working at my grandmother's plastic-bag factory. He was in his twenties and would sometimes come in to check up on the workers.

One day, however, barely anyone came down to check because my father was getting engaged to a women named Sokem. The marriage had been arranged by my grandfather. It was also a happy day for my mother, because after work my grandmother summoned her upstairs, where she was given an entire container of roast pork to take home to her family.

The previous year, when all the Chinese schools were closed

down, my mother had loitered with a gang of twelve-year-olds who haunted wealthier districts and let the air out of car tyres. She also went into an alleyway to try her first and last drag of a cigarette, and later, when her brother bought a motorbike, she "borrowed" it for rides when he was out.

My father had a distinctly different childhood – he studied French and classical guitar, went to the countryside to catch pet puppies, slid down the wooden banisters of the stairs in his triple-storey factory-house, swam in the river, climbed palm trees four times his height and practised acupuncture on volunteer patients after a two-week course in China.

But then Pol Pot's army swarmed into Phnom Penh like angry black ants and cleared the stage. My mother and her family escaped to Vietnam, while my father and his family were sent to the Killing Fields.

When they met again, it was more than half a decade later. She was selling material in the market-place in Saigon. She would wake up at four in the morning to go on that long, long walk to the village to buy fabric. When she arrived at the market, she would set up her stall and lay the pieces of material on the table. She learned slowly how to count in Vietnamese: "*môt, hai, ba, bôn, năm, sáu ...*", how to discern whether a customer was going to buy a piece of material, and how to bargain a buyer down.

During the war the women worked, while the men seemed to fade into insignificance. Women were in the market-place selling things and buying things. Women cooked at home, set up stalls and smacked their kids. Their husbands might have rode their bicycles to pick them up after work, or sat by their wives at the stall counting the money, but they seemed the tack-on helpers. My Outside Ma sold rice-cakes. My mother and Aunt Ly sold cloth. Aunt Bek worked cleaning houses, and my eldest uncle sold movie tickets. Anyone who could work in the family worked, and they pooled their money to live from day to day.

"Four years in Cambodia under Pol Pot," my mother told me, "and your father emerged looking like a brown skeleton." At first, my mother didn't recognise him at all. She and my Aunt Ly had sold their material and were sitting around eating noodles. Ly suddenly pointed past my mother's ear and exclaimed, "Oy, isn't that Little Aunt?"

Even though they had left the plastic-bag factory a long time ago, the respectful name Little Aunt still stuck when they talked about my Aunt Que. But the skinny girl Ly was directing her finger at was so thin and scruffy! How could it possibly be Que with the hair once so shiny that it had matched her school shoes?

"Ay, Little Aunt!" Ly called.

The young woman turned around and saw my mother and her younger sister. She looked at them both for a very long while, as if trying to match childhood faces to unfamiliar new grown-up figures. "Ah Ly!" she mouthed in astonishment, "Ah Kien! Wah, so you are in Vietnam! What about the rest of your family?" After Ah Pot's revolution, people from the Land of the Golden Tower no longer greeted each other with "Have you eaten yet?" No, now it was "Who is left in your family?"

"Our family is all here in Vietnam!" Ly proclaimed. "What about Old Auntie?"

"My mother is here too," said Que.

"Wah, that is just too good, too good!"

"And my brother is just over there!" In the middle of the market-place, she suddenly bolted off, yelling, "Brother, Brother! Guess who I found? You will never guess who is here!" She came back dragging some dumbfounded young man by the arm. When my mother looked at him, it made her think about how strange life was, that she and my Aunt Ly were here eating noodles and seeing their former bosses, all skin and bones, wide-eyed and bewildered like village folk having lost all their crops.

When my father saw my mother, he could not believe she was the same scrawny thirteen-year old operating the plastic-bag cutter. She was now twenty.

"Hey, you've grown up, Old Lady," he said to her, with a smile that almost split his face in half.

Even though surviving was what they were doing in Vietnam, my mother and father began to "walk together". Not alone, of course. Once my father went to the goldsmith and came back with a silver bracelet each for my mother and Aunt Ly. When Outside Ma found out, she exclaimed, "You be careful of this young man! A bracelet for each one of you! How very strange! You be careful that he is not one of those types of men who chase after two women at the same time!" But my mother knew the truth – she knew that my father really liked her but was too shy to make it clear. So he bought things for Ly too, because when they went out Ly was always trailing behind. My mother would ride on the back of my father's bicycle and they would try to lose her. The more agitated Ly became, the more fun they had.

Meanwhile, on the other side my grandmother was scared to death that my father liked Ly. Every time Ly came over to visit, my grandmother would give her the itchy eyeball glare.

Although Ly had her charms, all my grandmother could see was that she couldn't sit still and wore bright yellow stilettos in the strappy, ankle-snapping style of the era. "Kuan's mother doesn't like me," Ly told my mother matter-of-factly. It didn't bother her much.

"If you didn't dress like such a shiny red *Ung Bao* package, maybe she would stop it," my ma suggested helpfully.

"Hmmmph!" she said, "I am only enduring the insufferable atmosphere of that house because you are my sister. And this is what I get in return!"

*

One day, my mother came to return my father's bicycle. If she had known that someone else was present, she would not have come. The evening before, she had gone out with my father and he had given her his bicycle to ride home because it was getting very late. "You can return it to me in the morning," he told her.

So there she was, at the front of his house, with his bicycle. She saw an unfamiliar pair of shoes at the front doorstep. Pale blue with closed toes and thick heels. She thought that Aunt Que might have had a friend over. But they were unfamiliar shoes, and she knew all Que's friends. She didn't have many, because she could not speak much Vietnamese, and my grandmother clung tightly to her in case she learned of the depravities of Saigon from charming dope dealers.

Que opened the door. My mother told her, "Little Aunt, I have come to return your brother's bicycle."

"Ah Kien, come in! Come in!" she enthused. "Don't bother about taking off your shoes!"

"No, Little Aunt," my mother said, "I don't want to bother you when you have visitors."

Que looked down at the blue shoes on the doormat, noticing that my mother had noticed. "No! No! It's alright. Come in and have a little sit," she insisted.

"Who's that?" my mother heard my father's voice from inside the house. Then he muttered to someone inside the house, "just a moment," and appeared at the door.

"Um, brother, here is your bicycle," she said to him. Except at that very moment, she didn't feel like gracing him with "brother" this or that – she had heard the "just a moment" from inside and knew that he had been chatting with the owner of the blue shoes.

Turning to leave, she thought how stupid she was, thinking that a man nine years older was falling madly in love with her. After all, she was younger than his little sister Que.

"No, it's no bother, please come in," he insisted.

"No, really, I'd better go and not be a nuisance." But in all honesty, she was filled with curiosity. She wanted to see what this new girlfriend of his was like. She knew it was wrong to go in, and she knew her mother would yell, "Don't you have any shame, girl?" if she ever found out.

In the end, it was my grandmother who decided for her. She came out to see what the fuss was all about. "Ah Kien, you are here!" she exclaimed.

"Yes, Old Aunt," my mother muttered, keeping her eyes lowered, which also unfortunately meant that she had to look directly at the blue shoes.

"Come in! Come in!" She had never seen a family more adamant for her to come in and drink their tea before.

"Um, my mother is expecting me home soon."

But my grandmother had already grabbed my mother's arm and was leading her inside.

*

And then my mother saw her in the living room, sitting in the chair opposite my father. There she was, still smelling of newly pressed hair and sweet chemicals, a fresh perm on her head with two black pieces that curled like little crescent moons on her high cheekbones. She obviously had mascara on, thought my mother. No one could have eyelashes that long, just like the eyelashes on one of those wah-wah dolls. She wore a dress with a high collar and big buttons down the front, but no sleeves. Her skinny ankles were crossed, her hands were in her lap, and her back was straight.

My mother suddenly felt young and foolish, just like those people the popular love songs were always mooning on about. Her hair was a mess from the bicycle ride. "Oh," she said to my grandmother when she saw the other woman, "oh, uh, err, Old Aunt, I see you have visitors. So I will leave and not bother you now." She didn't want to admit it to herself, but she was jealous. She was furious, too, at my father, because he had told her to come today. She wanted to smash that bike of his. She decided that she would leave and give it a big kick as she walked away from that house, and never look back. Perhaps she could even puncture the tyre with the sharp end of her shoe.

"Oh no, don't leave," my grandmother said to my mother. "Take a seat, take a seat, Kien. I am sure Sokem doesn't mind!" When my mother realised who the visitor was, she froze. Sokem! All the muscles of her face pulled downwards. So that was the meaning of all this! How had she ended up here, my mother wondered. Ah, men, she thought, such liars! Such cheats! Her mother was right.

Now Sokem had come back to claim what was hers, and the fun for my father was over. They were going to fulfil my grandfather's wishes and go ahead with the arranged marriage.

During Ah Pot's terrible years, my grandfather had died of starvation. He had set off with his first wife when those black thieves the Khmer Rouge evacuated the city, and he had been allocated to a different work camp. It was a terrible journey, a parade of the desperate and the dying. The further they walked from the city, the more money flowed in the streets. But it was all useless, and banknotes would float through the air to fall uncollected into the dust. Cars were driven halfway and then dumped in ditches. Luckily, my mother's parents were clever enough to veer off the path one night and lead the family into Vietnam. Otherwise, like Sokem's parents, they would have died under Pol Pot.

Before they died, Sokem's parents told her that they had left some gold buried for her in the house, and that she should go back and look for it when the war was over. After the Killing Fields, Sokem miraculously found her old house – it had not been levelled – and dug up the gold. She then set off with her servant and young niece – the only survivor in her family – to look for my father.

But when my mother sat down, my father pulled his chair closer to her, away from his fiancé. Then my mother realised what was what. My grandmother also said to Sokem, "Ah Sokem, this is Kuan's friend, Kien." She introduced my mother as my *father's* friend instead of Aunt Que's friend. She said to my mother, "Ah Kien, how is your mother? Is she well? I have not visited her in a while." My grandmother was very good at putting bones in her words, bones to make the other person choke.

But Sokem was a lady, and she did not gasp and splutter. She still sat very straight, her face a stone mask, but the corners of her mouth dropped. She realised that my grandfather was dead, as well as her own parents, and that there was nobody left to enforce the promise my father's family had made half a decade ago. My mother could not look at her.

"Ah, it was good of you to visit us today, Sokem," my grand-mother said, standing up. "Good to see that you are well." Sokem slowly uncrossed her ankles. As my grandmother walked her to the door, Sokem muttered, "I am going, Old Auntie. Send my regards to Kuan and your family."

My parents could hear my grandmother saying to her, "Take care, Sokem, take care." And then the door closed, and Sokem was outside the house, but my mother was still inside.

I AM in my parent's wedding photos, with a lolly in my hands. My parents stand behind a table of oranges. Behind them is a double happiness character cut out of red paper stuck on the wall with glue. In her wedding photos, my mother is wearing Aunt Que's wedding dress and my father is in one of his grey suits with the wide trouser legs and small '70s lapels. It is a wedding for show, but there are not many people at the show. The only attendees are my grandmother, my Aunt Que and her new husband, Uncle Suong. All my mother's dreams of being the beaming bride are condensed into one spontaneous afternoon in our rented Footscray house in a borrowed dress, and only because someone came up with the bright idea of posing my parents for pictures among the residues of Aunt Que's wedding. My mother carries a fake bouquet of flowers in her lace-gloved hands.

All this to cover up the fact that there was no wedding back in Cambodia. No ceremony, no festivity. Not even an engagement period. From my parents' accounts it sounds like they were married in the bustling tedium of an ordinary day in Vietnam, wearing the best clothes they could find, which were no more than ordinary; but I like to think that their real marriage occurred in the darkness of the night, a night of visiting both sets of parents before setting off to find a way out of

Southeast Asia. Everyone knew that Thailand was the place with the refugee camp, the place that got people out of this bombed country and into one of those other democratic countries where you could buy Coca Cola in cans and not in plastic bags, where you could even throw the precious cans away.

Before my father asked my mother to marry him, he knew he had to have something to offer her, something more than a ride on the back of a bicycle or a silver bracelet. Yet what he had to offer was not something tangible, like a gold ring, or even a house in which to live. All he could offer her was a promise, something for her to picture in her imagination. It was quite a feat, to offer such an intangible, especially when he could not even call up any images out of which to construct this dream. It left a lot to the vagaries of her mind, and everything to her imagination.

He told her that he was heading to Thailand. He told her that he was getting forms processed for himself, his mother and his sister, Que. My mother saw him with American dollars in his pockets and a new Chinese-American wife, and they would both spit out the English like broken bones, spit it out like the way he was spitting out this existence here and now.

She tried to pretend that she didn't care. "When do you plan to go?" she asked.

"I'm going to get the forms processed this week," he said. If he was waiting for her to cry, she thought, then he would have to wait until the ancestors got up and started dancing jigs around them.

"I can make one for you too."

She didn't say anything.

"If you would like to come with me, then I will ask your

parents." And that is how my father proposed to my mother. There was no romantic melodrama, but I like to think that my mother, when she was young, had enough room for all the unknown pictures to grace the gallery of her mind, to have her vision framed by this moment of truthful sincerity.

They said their farewells to their families, and my outside grandparents gave them as many gold jewellery pieces as they could afford to part with. Then my parents set off on foot with my Aunt Que and my grandmother. They walked through the jungles of Vietnam and Cambodia, often sleeping on the bare ground at night, finally reaching Thailand.

There they spent one hot, sleepy year in the refugee camp.

There was no starvation at the camp. There was much waiting – at the food queue with bowls in hands, at the well with buckets on backs, on mats on the floor waiting, waiting, waiting. And in this long hot listless wait, I came into existence, made my mother's stomach swell up so that from sideways she looked like a long standing papaya.

My parents watched as my mother's stomach grew rounder, and wondered whether the child would come during Christmas in the camp, and if so, they knew that this child would squander their chances of getting out, of going overseas, for at least another year. They could be stuck in the camp for over half a decade. The refugee building was more of a wooden shack of many levels, made colourful by the kind-hearted Christian aid agencies and their festive cheer, their persistence in bringing light and life into the lives of those stunned into catatonia by darkness and death.

During that year, my father studied English in a small shack with a Vietnamese teacher so that he would have a better chance of getting out. My grandmother had taught him that with study, anything was possible; and that even though everything might be lost, there was always learning to bring about a redemption. And although my mother only had one month to go before her firstborn would come, her stomach looked three months younger.

When the family were finally accepted as refugees, my father was asked, "Canada or Australia?"

He knew nothing about either country, except that Canada had snow. So Australia it was.

PART III

"AH!" My mother's eyes flung open like shutters. It was early in the morning, or late in the night, or at that stage where it is neither morning nor night. She shot up in bed and looked at my father. "I know what the matter is now!" she cried, "why I can't find peace in this house!" Her hand nudged my father on the shoulder. "Ay, old man, wake up, wake up, I've found an answer!"

My mother had been having nightmares ever since we moved into our new house. She lay awake, tormented by on-again, off-again sleep, and could find no peace. "Aaarghhh," she would moan, clutching her heart in the mornings, "my heart is jumping to death." When she told me this, I had an image of the Jump Rope for Heart mascot in primary school, a red squirty shape skipping to near collapse inside her chest.

My father opened his eyes slowly. He groaned.

"Aiiiee," wailed my mother, "it is so glaringly obvious to me now why we have been having all these troubles! I can't understand why we failed to see it before!"

"Ahhhh," my father muttered, "I am so tired. Tell me about it and then let me rest!" His hands went to his eyes, his thumbs digging into the hollows at the corner of each socket and moving in small circular motions. This was his wake-up massage, learned from his acupuncture training in China when he was sixteen.

"It's our toilet!" said my mother fervently. "It's our toilet!"

My father's hands stopped moving. Had my mother gone dingdong? "Which one?"

"Our toilet! In this room! The ensuite toilet!" cried my mother. "That's the answer to the problems I have been having!"

"What do you mean?"

"I just had a dream," cried my mother, "about our Buddhist shrine, you know, the one downstairs with your father's picture on it! Aiyoh, how could we be so stupid as to put the family shrine in such a place?"

"Hah?" My father was befuddled. "I thought we agreed that the study was the best place, no kids coming to whack Ah Bah's photograph off the shelf!"

"No, no, no!" cried my mother, "you don't understand! The shrine downstairs is *directly below* our toilet upstairs! That's why I have been having such troubles! That's the reason!" We were crapping on our gods and ancestors. That was why there was no peace in this new house, why my mother clutched her heart every day and complained of the largeness of everything. Once we moved the shrine to a more auspicious place, all her troubles would be alleviated.

*

Dreams about ancestors and gods were serious matters, to be discussed over the breakfast table or over dinner. "Last night," my father would say, "I had a dream about Ah Bah. It is not right for me to go back to Cambodia this year." My father had been saying that for the past one and a half decades. Ah Bah's ghost, the ghost of my solemn-faced grandfather, was still floating around in the Mekong, molecules of his soul extending as far as Melbourne, warning my father not to go back. After a while, my father began to abandon his plans to follow in the footsteps of Uncle Pheang, who already owned six banks in Cambodia and went everywhere in a black bulletproof four-wheel drive with four bodyguards. Since there was no going back now, there was only one way for our little nuclear family to go and that was forwards. Forwards to the Great Australian Dream.

I thought about how my grandmother had saved up the profits from her plastic-bag factory to build her triple-storey terrace house in Phnom Penh. A week before they were to move in, Ah Pot's men were swarming across the city, and a week later all the residents of Phnom Penh were prodded into the countryside to work or die, or in most cases work *and* die.

Now in this new country, my father was in a position to build his own dream home, in a location untainted by bad dreams and ominous paternal warnings. Every evening for a month, we pored over the details of how exactly our new house was to be built, this house with popping-out bay-window eyes, in muted hues of cream and white. We squished together on the floor in my parent's bedroom in our Braybrook home, heads bent over plans, fingers pointing here, there and every-where. "Such a big house for such little people," my friends commented.

As the house was being built, my father took his only day off work to drive us to its foundations. This was our weekly Sunday trip, to watch the temple being constructed and to worship the fruits of our labour. My thirteen-year-old brother and I walked on the set-concrete foundations, through the wooden-plank doorways and wahhed over the wooden-beam skeleton of the house, reckoning where the rooms would be and marvelling at the largeness of it all. After about ten minutes, we were thoroughly bored, but my parents would still be walking through the wooden ribcage of the house, hand in hand, looking up up and up towards where the upstairs area would be. And they would comment to each other on where things were going in the new house, comparing it to our neighbour Danny's.

Meanwhile, my sister Alina would squish her four-year-old feet into the mounds of soil dug up at the front, and later, the mountains of sand. She would smile her perfect-toothed, dribbly-chinned grin and fall on her hands. She would pick up half-empty chip packets the builders had left behind and shove the contents in her mouth if we weren't looking, or collect Coke cans and the contents would pour down her front when we tried to snatch them away from her. Alison, who was seven, was more collected. She would walk up and down the mountain of building sand, careful not to step on nails. She would also stack small blocks of wood, building replica palaces for the indifferent ants. My mother put my sisters in dresses for these outings, though it was not as if we were going to church. I suppose she was practising for the time when we would move into this new life, a life of navy-blue and white tailored dresses and Mary-Jane shoes.

*

Before we moved, my mother packed away the colourful dresses and tracksuits with their little embroidered cotton patches of puppies and girls with woollen braids and appliquéd cat faces on the front. She stuffed them into a swollen orange plastic Brotherhood of St Laurence bag to be shipped off to those new Fresh-off-the-Boats-and-Planes who would, we hoped, marvel over them with the same awe and seemingly everlasting gratitude that we once had. Gone now were the days where a one-dollar plastic brown vinyl coat was a birthday present from the government.

Now we could exchange our old clothes for new, and we could look at the recently arrived ones, noting their grey tights with yellow dresses and velcro shoes, and we could roll our eyes and think that although they didn't know any better now, they would learn, oh they would learn to adapt or be laughed at. But they were the ones who were laughing, and oh how they laughed, with their mouths wide open and their eyes shut tight, and when they were not laughing they were walking around with their eyes wide open and their mouths shut tight taking it all in – all the things that we had taken in a decade ago. And we felt pity and resentment and plenty of embarrassment for their eagerness and their countryside errors. But most of all, unacknowledged envy of their pure, rooted-to-the-moment, everyday-is-a-wonderland existence, because it reminded us of a distant self we once were, we of the wide-eyed, shut-mouth stupor, we of the wide-mouth, shut-eyed delirium, when things were louder and funnier and lettuce was greener and gleaming concrete seemed newer.

*

When we moved into the new house, there were no more paper-chains from the Target advertisements strung up from the stipple-dot plaster ceiling. How could we even imagine sticky-taping the clean white walls with our painted-macaroni works of junk? Things needed to be different, things were whitewashed. Nothing could look too peasanty. No dark wooden furniture, but rather white and peach and pale green. Family came to visit, not to celebrate but to do the tour so that they could get home-furnishing ideas for their own houses, so that they too would look modern and not too peasanty. They did not even sit down long enough to have a cup of tea, or if they did, their conversation would always turn to the New House. "How much per square metre?" "Where did you get the glass table?" "Did the builder try and rip you off?"

After seeing our place, Aunties Que and Anna bought land in the area too – Aunt Que immediately across the road from us, with the Maribyrnong River as her back view; and Aunt Anna behind our house so that we were neighbours. When my grandmother's Buddhist monk came from Vietnam to visit her, she brought him to our house to bless it. Even though our property was an irregular skirt shape, he lauded my father's fine choice. All the feng shui elements of our house were in balance, and it was to be a place of much happiness.

"Do not build your house on a hill where the back slopes down," advised the monk, "because all your luck is going to slip down that hill." And so my Auntie Que sold her property before she could even plan for architects to come and have a look at the land, and she moved away from us.

Aunt Anna, on the other hand, stayed where she was – the monk had said that her land was good. My father helped her with the architectural plans, and within a year another Avondale Heights mansion had arisen. Around us were palaces with Don smallgoods trucks parked at the front or white panel vans to carry the bolts of fabric or dumpling pastries to the factories in which family members worked. And work they did, for we would only see the vans and trucks parked in their driveways very late at night, or very early in the morning when we were heading off to school to embark on our own first steps in fulfilling the dream.

*

Yet there was still a piece missing. My mother could feel it, even after we moved the Buddhist shrine away from the room beneath my parents' upstairs ensuite toilet. The Jump Rope for Heart mascot was still hammering away in her chest, and in the mornings she would wake up with black crescents under her eyes. Even so, she would wake up at six or seven and set about her work. When all else stopped, physically, mentally and spiritually, work was her only constant, the life-raft she built with whatever little life spark she had left in her.

The second revelation came, as dramatic as the first, yet to act on it was no easy matter. "I know why I have been feeling this way!" she cried, shooting up in bed a second time. She couldn't find the little glass jars of gold she had buried in the backyard when we first moved to our old house in Braybrook; the jars of gold we kept as a residue of the fear left from the old country – the fear that money could so easily become worthless pieces of dirty paper, and the conviction that the only permanent security was gold. "We haven't dug them up yet!" she cried. "I remember there being four more jars of gold we haven't dug up yet!"

"Are you sure it exists?" asked my father. "Are you sure?"

But she could not remember. "But I had the dream," my

mother said, "and in my dream, I remembered we buried them!"

"Are you sure you didn't turn them into jewellery to sell?"

"I can't remember, but I can't have been feeling this way for so long for nothing! There has to be a reason, and if it is not the shrine being in the wrong place, it is our gold being in the wrong place!"

My father's ears were getting irritated and tired, and he had to think about his business meeting the next day with the suppliers from Hitachi. "Well, how are we going to get the gold back from the new owners of the Braybrook house hah? As if they are going to let us come over and dig up their back-yard for jars of gold!"

"That Cantonese Chicken Market lady!" lamented my mother. "She works in Footscray and she doesn't even remember to return our mail to us! Woe, how are we ever going to get the gold back?" My mother thought about the endless suffering ahead if the gold was not dug up, and she sighed her ten-thousand-sorrows sigh. All that hard work, all that effort – buried and forgotten!

Finally, my parents devised a plan. They *would* go back to the old Braybrook home, and they *would* dig up the backyard. And of course, the Chicken Market lady would let them in.

"Aiyah, aiyah, of course you can come!" urged the new owners of our old house when my mother called and told them what she needed to do. "Come as soon as you can!" The Chicken Market lady's voice was throbbing with anxiety. She was scared to death of the ancestors, everybody was. My mother had told her that she needed to go back to dig up the remains of her ancestors from the terrible years in the old country.

They were unquietly resting in urns buried throughout the backyard.

While it was my father who had concocted the plan with my mother, it was actually my Auntie Anna and my mother who executed it. Equipped with shovels, incense and bulldust Buddhist mantras, they knocked on the familiar front door. "Cut down our plum tree at the front," muttered my mother to my auntie.

The Chicken Market lady did not welcome my ma and my aunt into the house, but instead told them that she would open the gate leading to the backyard for them – "more convenient". "She just doesn't want ancestor-diggers in her new house," muttered my mother.

When my ma and aunt came into the backyard, they noticed that our old lemon tree was still in its corner, with its lemons hanging from the limbs like big bright yellow eyeballs watching without blinking.

My ma lit incense sticks and bowed in various places in the backyard before sticking the sticks in the ground. My auntie stood over them and recited Buddhist prayers. These incense stalks were little markers for those coveted pots of gold. They burned in the wind, and the orange glow went out of some of them, but they were not relit. There was no time.

The sky was grey so my ma and aunt set to work quickly with their shovels, while Chicken Market lady stood by. "Did you find it yet? Did you find it yet?" she kept asking anxiously. Later, as the sky began to spit rain, she watched from our old kitchen window as my auntie and my mother dug holes in her backyard.

The souls of seven dead kittens were dug up in the process,

and old childhood toys with the plastic palely discoloured. A lot of stones and rocks and stubborn grass-roots clung to the dirt, so they dug, deeper and deeper, and the incense sticks burned out one by one in the wind. Finally, when all the markers had been explored, and the holes had been made, my mother dropped the shovel.

"Didn't find anything," my mother sighed, her hands hanging limply at her sides. The Chicken Market lady flung her hands up to her head. *No, this cannot be!* she wanted to cry, *get these disturbing ancestors off my property. Try harder, dig some more!* But then she took one look at my mother's face, black crescents beneath the eyes, rain-soaked and steeped in defeat, and she kept her mouth shut.

"**K** I M" was both the Vietnamese and the Chinese word for gold, so all the jewellery shops were called Kim Heng or Kim Huang or Kim Ngoc, depending on the family name of the owners. These little shops epitomised Family Business, and there were so many of them down the shopping strips of St Albans, Springvale, Richmond and Footscray that I had trouble remembering their names, so that they melded into one continuous never-ending counter filled with red velvet and 24-carat gold. The owners of the jewellery stores I herded into one collective noun – the Kims. One Kim had her daughter's dental surgery above her shop. Another Kim had two sons working there. A third Kim wore make-up like the actors in *Farewell My Concubine* and painted her eyebrows three centimetres above her real eyebrows, or where her real eyebrows would have been if she had not plucked them out.

One day after school I went with my mother while she did her round of visiting the Kims. I was still in my school uniform, and my mother let me collect the money for her, put it in a used white envelope and double-check that it was the right amount. "Look how much I make," she told me proudly as I counted the $50 and $100 bills. "All in one day." Yet I knew it was not all from one day's work. It was weeks and weeks of labour. It was just that the pay all came at once, when she did her rounds of the shopping strips. "This is my daughter," she told all the Kims. "My daughter is in Year Eleven. She is going to become a lawyer." *Hey* – since when was I going to become a lawyer? Even I hadn't decided that yet. It was because I was terrible at maths, my mother told me in the car afterwards, and had no way of ever becoming a doctor. She secretly hoped that one of the Kims' sons was studying to be a doctor.

The Vietnamese lady Kims made themselves look very attractive. They painted their faces with powder and foundation and sometimes the hue did not match their necks, but that didn't matter once you saw the face. The Chinese lady Kims, on the other hand, seemed less chic. They had tight perms and an earthiness about them, a turnip-and-carrot-soup sort of existence. Their lives, like my mother's, seemed removed from their gold. They worked for the gold, but they did not own the gold – the gold owned them. What were they working for? What indeed? They did not work to prettify themselves, they did not work for the status and prestige because it was dirty work, it was work with dangerous chemicals and blackened fingertips. They worked for their children, and when you are a child with parents killing themselves with dangerous chemicals just so you can live a comfortable life, there is no comfort within, just a gnawing guilt only to be alleviated by being at the shop after school, helping your parents read the stacks of letters and bills and notifying them of their business registration renewals. The kiddie Kims grew up fast, they had business acumen inculcated in them early. Meanwhile, the Mr Kims only made special appearances at the shopfront to deal with a difficult customer or to count the gold. They usually sat at the back of the store with files and surgeons' scalpels, making more jewellery or adjusting customer purchases – fixing wedding and engagement rings that were too wide, or bracelets that were too loose. They also polished the pieces to a gleaming yellow and did a whole host of other things I did not see or understand.

Sometimes the Kims would do runners, those that were going bankrupt. One week they would accept wares from my mother, the next week they were nowhere to be seen, their stores had closed down and the windows were covered in newspaper. Such a shame to go bankrupt, that was why they told nobody – but it also meant that they did not have to pay off their debts to the outworkers. My mother could not stand debtors who made false promises.

One time, some Kims owed her and had not paid for many months. So she paid them a visit. She brought in a big old coat and a bread bun in a plastic bag and sat in the chair reserved for customers. She waited patiently until the Kims were done serving their customers. They tried to ignore her. More customers came in. She still waited. In between intervals of customers, she told the Kims she was waiting for her payment. She waited until closing time. The other Kims from the block and from the other suburbs' stores had warned my mother that this Kim was going bankrupt, that they were soon closing down because Mr Kim loved Crown Casino too much.

"We can't pay you yet," the Lady Kim said. "We don't have the money."

"That's what you always say, sister."

"But this time we really can't!"

"Well, I am going to wait here until you can pay me," my mother said. "Because I am not coming home tonight without my pay. You haven't paid me for three months. My husband will think I wasted all those hours of my life doing the work. I will be too ashamed to go home without the money."

"Well, there is nothing we can do about that," said Mrs Kim. "As I told you, we have no money." She could see my mother looking at her cases and cases of gold.

"Chinese people shouldn't owe any debts," said my mother.

"Come on, we are going bankrupt! Our house is going to be sold," entreated Mrs Kim as she started packing up all her trays of jewellery, hoping my mother would get the message.

"Why don't you go home?" Mr Kim beseeched her.

My mother started to unwrap her bread roll. "Can't," she said. "Not until I get paid."

"Well, you can't stay in our store!"

"You just pack up and don't mind me. You can go home but I am going to stay here overnight." She leaned back in her chair.

In the end, frustrated and feeling sorry for her, the Mr Kim took out a gold bracelet from his tray and told her, "We're going to give you jewellery for surety until we can get the money to pay you back." My mother watched as he carefully measured the bracelet on the scales to make sure it weighed as much as my mother was owed.

When my mother got home that evening, she showed us the bracelet. It even had little cubic zirconias in it. Two months later, when the debt-owning Kims sold their store, they called my mother up to tell her that they had money for her. She returned the bracelet and collected the money.

Perhaps the Kims did not know enough about the Australian law to figure out that outworkers were not subject to protection in debt matters. We all came from countries where the laws were scattered and broken, and where they could be bought with bribes, where wars happened and currency was rendered worthless at the flash of a bomb, so that the only dependable commodity of trade was gold. The Kims were used to trading on the basis of word of honour, so this became our business protocol. And when the word was not honoured, the worker was all alone. Most of the Kims were decent people; and, locked out of the language of the outside world, they knew they had only their outworkers to keep them in business. No sane Australian would be willing to work under such conditions, for so little. And yet, the dollar they paid kept dropping.

"Ten dollars a ring? You have got to be kidding me!" The Kim flung up her hands in horror.

"But that's how much I always charge for the ones with the stones in them."

"No, I can get it from that new man from Vietnam. He only charges eight dollars."

My mother would leave to go to another store. But then she found out that the new man from Vietnam had been there too. She would then have to come back to the first store and try to bargain them up.

"Nine dollars then."

"Come on, you have got to be joking. Move with the times."

"My craftsmanship is better."

"Yeah? Look at this." The Kim held out a ring for her to take a look. It was polished with no strokes of the jade polisher, all even and shining. It was good craftsmanship, but more importantly the new man from Vietnam had superior technology. He had a machine.

"Okay. Eight dollars-fifty then. Eight-fifty is my final offer."

"Come on, you don't need the money. Your husband owns the two Hi-Fi stores."

That was the excuse they now all used. You don't need the money. Your husband owns two Hi-Fi stores.

In fact, you don't need to work at all.

This was their power over her, which they thought they were only using to undercut her. After all, business was business. They did not realise that they were also stripping away her sense of purpose. She calculated that she still had twenty-five years of working life left. If she had no work, what would she do with those years?

An outsider looking in would see myriad options. Why doesn't she go to school and learn English? We had enough money now that she didn't need to work. Why didn't she start a small business? Most ridiculous of all, why didn't she take it easy and live a life of luxury?

*M*Y mother was not a talker, she was a shouter. The worst shouting was in the car with my auntie. Scared of not being heard, she would hurl out her sentences, punctuating them with exclamation marks. Each sentence was loud and grating, and when she got to talking about people she did not like, oh God, you would need earplugs if you were in the car, or a very loud Walkman, and you would have to conceal the wires of the headphones underneath your scarf, cover your ears with your hair. Nod nicely and look intensely as if you were listening. She would start off talking normally, and then get louder and louder, until the whole conversation turned into a screaming match without an argument, just statements about where were the cheapest Flying Dragon vegetables and instant Indo Mie noodles. Cursed be the soul who tried to contradict her. The less she had to say, the louder she got. "Three ninety-nine! I have been shopping for twenty years, I would know a cheap ten-pack of toilet paper if I saw it! None can buy as cheaply as me!"

"But for four-fifty ..." her sister would begin.

"Four-fifty!" scoffed my mother, "four-fifty is stupid, four-fifty is fifty cents more!" My mother's motto was never to pay full price for anything, and bargain-hunting for us did not mean going to the half-price sales, it meant rummaging through the shop-soiled and cast-off trolley at Target.

But you could not buy an education for half-price. "How is a $115 wool jacket supposed to help one study better hah?" my mother demanded as I clambered into the back of the car after school. I had no idea about the correlation between wearing a blazer and academic brilliance either, but she wasn't talking to me, she was talking to my Aunt Bek, who was in the passenger seat.

"Not every family can send their kids to such a school, you know," my mother said pointedly to her oldest sister. "Especially not the girls."

"No, of course not," my Auntie Bek agreed. Especially not if your husband worked at the Arnotts biscuit factory.

"When we were growing up, we didn't have such opportunities. We went to work when our school closed down. Do you remember when they closed down our Chinese school?"

"Young people these days, so fortunate hah," said my auntie. "They know so much. Soon they will be smarter than we are!"

"No!" retorted my mother. "They spend their whole lives at school and instead of making them brighter, it makes them limp and lazy. She's always got her face stuck in some book. And you'd think with all that education, they would at least know the simplest things, but they don't. I tell her to look at the bank statements and explain them to me, but she can't."

I sat slumped in the back seat of the car. It was true, I couldn't. It wasn't that I couldn't understand the English, it was that I didn't have the Chinese terms in me to be able to explain. I was running out of words.

When our car pulled into the driveway, I slouched into the room, feeling incongruous and imperial in my fancy uniform and royal-blue hair ribbons, hands with calluses only from writing, not from hard manual work. At the new school, I never said a word in class unless the teacher picked on me. One wrong word could mean being found out for the philistine that I was. The quieter I became at school, the louder my mother became at home. She was loud because she could not read or speak the secret talk we knew. She could not read because she had been housebound for two decades. And now, over the dinner table, she would watch as my father and his children littered their language with English terms, until every second word was in the foreign tongue. We hardly noticed the food which she had prepared for us, so engrossed were we in our babble. She sat there staring at us, trying to make sense of these aliens at her table.

"Migrants don't assimilate," I was told by classmates in politics class. "They all come here and stick together, and don't bother to learn the language." But I remembered when my mother bundled all four of us into the car after school. "Agheare," she told me, "look up the map. Find this place for me. Your father gave me the address. I am going to learn the English. I am going to learn it now, no matter what." We did not even change out of our uniforms, there was no time. My mother decided that if she knew the English, all her problems would be solved, she would be able to do anything in this new country. Most of all, she would be able to enter the world of her children's minds. We pulled up in front of a community centre and were met by a kind woman with a lilting British accent, hair like a soft grey felt hat on her head, grey flannel scarf and kind grey eyes. She looked like an old wise possum and she invited us all into the centre for coffee before our discussion.

My mother's heart melted. We all sat down around a table strewn with newspapers and books.

"So it says here that your mother is forty?" said the woman incredulously.

Until then, I didn't even know my mother's age. I asked her, and she nodded.

"Unbelievable! She looks twenty!"

I repeated this to my mother.

"Wow, forty and four kids," breathed the woman, looking around at each of us, "incredible." I didn't need to explain this to my mother. She signed up for the class straightaway. After all, it was only ten dollars a term – a bargain, she thought, and such a kind teacher too.

*

My mother asked us to speak to her in English. I did so, slowly and carefully. I asked her questions: "How are you? How was your day?" But because these were questions Chinese children never asked their parents, even if she had enough words to answer me, she would not have known how. "Stop asking me crazy pointless questions," she said, "and let me learn something useful!"

"Alright, Ma. What do you want to learn? What do you want to talk about?"

"You tell me! You're the teacher now!" She looked at me as if I had all the answers and was keeping them from her from some perverse whim, as if I had them hidden in the inside pocket of my blazer.

The migrants in her class were all at different levels, and my mother could not understand the worksheets with the fill-in-the-blanks about Ned Kelly. "So sick of sitting down with none of this making any sense!" she cried. "Who gives a crap about the man with the tin can over his head? Stupid idiot. As if that is going to help me understand how to speak useful things better!" She dumped all her notebooks and worksheets on the floor of her room. Never put your books on the floor, my grandmother warned me, or you won't do well in school, but I did not repeat this to my mother.

"Well, this stuff might be too hard," I said, discreetly shoving the piles of paper under her bed. "Why don't you start from the very beginning?" I picked up my five-year-old sister's school reader. "Pat is … a … Cat," my mother read. "He is a black and white cat." Her fingers, gnarled as just-dug-up ginseng, pointed at each word. She could read the whole book through not once, not twice, but three times.

She sighed a big sigh. "Ah, it's no use. No use! It is all useless! I don't understand a thing."

"But Ma, you just read the whole book through three times!"

"No, I didn't!"

"Yes, you did!"

She turned to the middle pages and pointed. "I don't know what it says. I can't sound out the words. I just memorised the whole thing when you first read it out to me. Don't teach me any more. Go off and study. I'm getting old, going blind, my working life is over, I can't even see well enough to be able to link these chains of the little gold bracelets together, I keep cutting myself. I am old, and I am going to be relying on you in the future. Go off and study."

Yet the more I studied at school, the more mute I became. I

lost so many words that there seemed no possibility of ever recovering them. Although I ticked "English as a second language" on all official forms, I was beginning to think in English. It was true, too, that the more I studied, the dumber I got. I could not even answer the simplest questions my mother posed of me. At least I was losing my word-spreading status, I thought – soon my mother might even forget that I had once told tales. Now there weren't even enough words to say how I was feeling, and all feeling was reduced to the simplest of three emotions: "I am happy", "I am sad" or "I am angry." My mother's moods alternated between the last two. She made the most of the words she still had by delivering them at ten million decibels in the car. "Woe and great suffering," she yelled. "You are all going to leave me. I am getting old and you are all going to leave me because I don't know the English!" Knowing the English became her obsession. She would ask us what certain words meant whenever she heard snatches from television. "Agheare, what is 'Spotlight'? Agheare, what are they saying in the movie?" She grew frustrated when she could not understand, when we could not translate, when we were too busy with a book in front of our face to bother telling her what stupid things like "Big M" meant. "Why is it called that?" "What meaning does it have?" "Why do the Australians call their milk that?" My mother's questions became more difficult to answer than the literature we had to study in class.

*

One day when I did not have school, I spent the day with my mother. She drove to my Aunt Bek's house. As we approached the front of the mock-Georgian house, she said, "Watch to see if the husband is home! Is that his car at the front? If he is home, we'd better drive off quick!" My mother was on one of her "rescue raids" again. I later found out that she conducted these raids often, after she had dropped us off to school. She would drive to my auntie's house and take her around to our house to talk and help her do housework, or she would help my aunt do her own housework. I checked to see if the red Corolla was in the driveway. "No, Ma," I replied, "the uncle is not at home." The uncle was Aunt Bek's husband. My aunt opened the door and let us in. The house was still and silent, with both her twin sons at school. It was as quiet as our house.

I realised then that it was the same everywhere. Inside these double-storey brick-veneer houses, countless silent women were sitting at their dining tables. They were living the dream lives of the rich and idle in Phnom Penh, and yet their imposed idleness made them inarticulate and loud. They didn't know how to live this life of luxury and loneliness. Used to working for others all their lives, they did not know how to be idle without guilt, and they could not stop working.

"How fortunate you are!" my mother said to my aunt. "Much luckier than I am. I suffer so much. My husband is always working and never drives me anywhere. On weekends all he wants to do is sweep the floor and sit around resting." But my auntie would have none of it. "I suffer much more than you do!" she cried. "At least your husband does the housework. At least you can drive. My husband won't let me drive anymore since I smashed into the tree-trunk of the telephone pole!" And on and on it went, a litany of lamentations about who had the worse state of affairs, culminating in the topic of Disappointing Children.

"Terrible, aiyoh, just terrible!" My auntie is telling a story. Her eyes widen and her mouth twists to prove a point about my twin cousins. "Can you believe sons like that? Useless! 'Hey Pa,' they say, 'you can let us off here. Don't drive in front of the school, I will walk from here!' After how Ah Buong worked to get them in that school, and in the first week they are ashamed of the car their father drives!"

"Aiyoh, they don't speak to me anymore!" continues my auntie. "When they come home from school, they just rush to their rooms and go on their com-pu-tahs. They can sit still for hours in front of the machines, and I don't know whether they are playing games or not!"

"Aiyohh, yours don't speak to you anymore? Well, I have it worse. Mine *can't* speak to me anymore!" lamented my mother as she raised one eyebrow towards me. "See that one there? She can't even string a proper sentence together!"

"At least you have a girl! A girl can keep you company when you are old." My auntie watched me at the wok, trying to fry up some taro cakes for lunch.

"Yes, but she's gone with the ghosts already. She's going to marry one, and then it will be the end of us. At least you have sons who can marry good Chinese girls, give you daughters-in-law who will listen to you, as daughters never do."

"We're doomed, we who do not know the English!" lamented my aunt, "doomed!"

Both my mother and my aunt sat at the dining-room table, submerged in their doom and gloom. "What woe it is not to know the English and to be depending on your useless children!"

"And when we grow old, they'll do what they do in this

country and cart us off to old people's homes! And we'll be stuck with the old white ghosts. Eating their food, their cheeses and other vomity things."

"How terrible!" This vision of nursing-home nausea so overwhelmed my mother and my auntie that they both turned their heads towards me.

"You won't let that happen to us, will you?" asked my aunt.

"Kids these days have no loyalty," sighed my mother. "When they get husbands, they are going to move far far away from us. It's no use digging up promises from them now. Just wait till they get older, they will follow their husbands. And we'll be like mutes! Wordless!" My mother's voice was rising.

"All women are mute and wordless when they have husbands," sighed my auntie.

"No, they get mute and wordless when they have mothers-in-law like mine!"

Both women looked at me, making sure I learned this important lesson.

"Agheare, you have to be fierce," my mother told me. "Not like us, always working for other people."

"But you can't be lazy either," my auntie told me. "Being lazy is the worst thing a woman can be."

"Aiyah, what's the use of teaching her these things when she is going to leave me anyhow? She is filled with foreign thoughts and she thinks these foreigners have all the answers!"

*

When I burned the taro cakes while frying them in the wok, I realised I knew nothing, that I could do nothing. That all this learning inside my head was of no use in life. "Aiyah, you don't squish them like that!" cried my mother, "Look. Watch. Just pour lots of oil in and swirl it around. Like this." She grabbed the metal stirrer from me and with a few deft flicks turned the cakes over. I watched in admiration.

"Ma, you need to teach me how to cook."

"You don't need to learn how to cook. When you get married, you're going to be making ghost food," she said, "for your ghost husband." She imagined future dinners for me, with boiled broccoli and mashed potatoes and slabs of meat, all seasoned with salt and pepper. She had given up on me! "What is the use of teaching you when you are going to leave me anyway?" she said. "You never listen to what I say."

If I listened to what she said, I would be one of those girls who could cook proper food, and would marry a nice Teochew boy and be sweet and obedient. If I listened to what she said, I would not be this woeful daughter with a head crammed full of foreign thoughts, only using Chinese to ask questions or get things: "What are we having for dinner?" "Did you get the money back that was owed you by Ah Kim Heng?"

Yet these questions were of no consequence. What were important were the big questions, the big questions we never asked each other, for lack of words. I watched my mother and her sister as they sipped tea while simultaneously wiping the kitchen table. I put the taro cakes in a plate and placed them on the table. As I watched them quietly eating the squashed and slightly burnt squares, with no words for my incompetence anymore, I wanted to cry.

Late in the afternoon, my mother drove Aunt Bek back in the car, getting back before her husband arrived home. "I saved her from spending the day sleeping in bed," my mother told me as we headed back home. "I saved her from being alone. And we got the floors wiped."

I remembered something. "Ma, didn't you have English lessons this morning?"

"What? Oh, English lessons. Stopped going."

"Why?"

"Who would I speak the English to, I ask you?"

I was silent in the back seat.

"IT'S drip-drip-dripping," said my mother. "The light is dripping with water-spirits." At least, that was what I heard her say. I looked up. The chandelier did droop with crystals. There must have been close to a hundred of them. I switched it on to see the full effect.

"Turn it off!" cried my mother. "What are you doing? Stupid, turning it on and off like that, wasting energy!" The chandelier was supposed to be saved for visitors. Just like the sitting room, with its cream leather sofas that were never used, and the glass dining table that had never seen a dinner on its surface.

I flicked off the switch because my mother's eyes were sunken and the skin around her sockets was like crumpled parchment paper. She had just woken up from her sleep. "Aiyyyah," she sighed, deep and slow. "Time to pick up the kids. Time to make dinner."

No, I wanted to tell her, it was *not* time to pick up the kids. That was over forty-five minutes ago. And it was *not* time to make dinner. It was four o'clock in the afternoon, for crying out loud.

"What time is it?" she asked me.

I told her.

"Bloody hell! 4.37! Why didn't you tell me? The kids are still at school waiting!"

"No, I picked them up on the way home." It was a one-and-a-half kilometre walk for them back home, because no buses ran up the hills of Avondale Heights. When I arrived at the school, my sisters were the last ones there – waiting outside closed office doors. Bobbing down beneath the grey sky in their green uniforms and brown socks, they dug small sticks into the dirt of the curb.

My mother's shoulders loosened, but they also slumped. Another failure on her part, she thought. Firstly she could no longer work, and secondly she could no longer look after her kids. All the things that my grandmother had predicted – or cursed – were coming true.

My mother had stopped working on the gold a few weeks ago. The chemicals were getting to her and making her cough, she told us. The coughs never seemed to get better. So no more familiar wax smells wafting from the other room to mingle with our toast and decaffeinated coffee in the morning. The room next to the kitchen, where my mother grew her wax trees, was dark. An old bedspread covered her work-table like a shroud.

*

"Your father told me to sell all my tools and machines, and live my life looking after the children and taking care of the house," she would tell me, as I sat in the study which also doubled as my mother's workroom. I was trying to write essays for my final-year high-school assessment. She sat slumped in her torn vinyl work-chair. "What do you think I should do?"

"It is so terrible," she continued. "I feel like a useless useless person now. Should I sell all my machines? Should I?" She looked deep into my eyes, something that Asian parents never do to their children – but she was desperate.

"I don't know." I tried to get my mind off the "Multi-tiered System of the Australian Judiciary" for a little while. I tried to be reasonable. I tried to put myself in her place. "Could you be happy not working?"

"No." Of course not. A stupid question.

"Then maybe you could just continue working."

"But Agheare, I am getting old! Getting old. I can't do this forever. How long will it last? Three years? Five years? I am too old to go running around Footscray and Richmond and Springvale with a bag filled with gold, always scared that someone will snatch it. I am too old to be working late into the night. My eyes – they are getting weaker and *moh-moh* blurry. Getting old, getting old! And this job – it will be the end of me! My end of days will come sooner than most people's end of days." My mother worked with dangerous chemicals – sulfuric acid, ammonia, gold-potassium cyanide. "Look! Look at my hands!" She held them out in front of her, fingers spread. They were cracked and blackened at the tips, almost as if they had been burnt. They were a coal-miner's hands, I realised.

"So much cleaning in the new house!" she cried, even though it was not the house that needed cleaning, it was her mind. "And no one ever helps!"

"I wish I could be like your aunties and work at the shop counting money. But I don't know the English!" she cried. And then she really cried, heaving heavy honking sobs. I sat still, my back straight. I had tried to comfort her once by putting my arms around her. She pushed me away. I learned never to do it again, so the only consolation I could offer was silence.

"What am I going to do? What am I going to do? I am a useless person!" she wailed. Alina stuck her little head around the door to see what was going on in the study.

"Go watch some TV," I commanded. "Go watch *George and Martha*."

"But I can't do my maths," she said.

"Go ask Alexander."

"But ..."

"Go *now*." I had learned to speak in orders. No other seventeen-year-old I knew, unless they were terribly spoilt, spoke in orders.

My mother wanted to stand in front of the shop and work at the till too, but she was shy, felt she did not know enough English, and always felt herself small against my father's family. After all, she had worked at their plastic-bag factory when she was thirteen, and thought she would be in their eyes forever thirteen and scrambling for scraps. This was a woman who knew at least five different languages fluently, yet who had not studied beyond Grade One when they closed down all the Chinese schools in Cambodia. She worked harder than anyone else I knew, but now that she had stopped working, everything was shattering around her – and with this force-field gone, she could also see all the lives happening around her. Inspiring things were happening to them, interesting things, things of hope and progress, and yet her own life was static. There was no going forward, except to be carried down by others, down down down deep and dark and forever. It was scaring the living daylights out of her.

She would drive her car to Dr Cheng's office and tell him, "Doctor, my heart is jumping out of my chest! I think I may be having a heart attack soon!" Dr Cheng listened to her, because she had nobody else to speak to. And doctors were meant to have answers. Dr Cheng told her that feeling this way was not uncommon, that she was not going crazy. He told her that it would be okay, from what little she revealed.

Depression, the doctor called it, but my mother did not know what that meant. "Scattered thoughts," she told Dr Cheng, "that's all they are, these crazy scattered thoughts. I think about all our money disappearing at the shop. I think of losing everything, and my heart thumps like crazy and it is unbearable!" Sickness in the heart, she said, a sickness in the heart that she needed to get checked out. It was physical, she reckoned, and once the doctors could give her some medicine for her heart thumping much harder than it should, then she would be closer to recovery. So the doctor gave her little white pills in a cardboard box with bold red writing. ZOLOFT. Take these twice a day, he told her. And wait. Be patient and wait. They will not work straightaway.

She could not stand to be in the house, in the house she could not stand still. It was so hollow, so many hours to fill, how could she fill them all by wiping down the fridge or washing the sheets? She would drive to the supermarket and do what she had always done – buy food on sale, look for the green fluorescent stickers; and at the register count out the exact amount in notes and coins. Our Asko side-by-side fridge with the ice dispenser would be packed with fast food that came two-for-price-of-one. But after a while, she did not even know what she was buying. She walked into the supermarket stunned, not because there was so much to be had, but because none of it made any sense now, or brought any happiness. She operated

156

like an automaton – first she would go to the trolley filled with broken CLEARANCE items, then she would find the SALE bread, or the discount day-old bread, and then any other miscellaneous things on SPECIAL. Once she brought home twenty 250-gram blocks of Nestlé chocolate in different flavours. "A dollar-fifty a block," she said. "Never seen such a price before." Without the energy or thought to hide them around the house, she left them in the cupboard above the oven rangehood. My siblings and I went though one and a half blocks a day each and she didn't even notice.

The only thing she became obsessive about was the house and the cleaning. A tiny little scratch on the wall or a splattering of oil on the granite would drive her to madness. Every muscle in her chest would tense, she would have no self-control. The furniture was driving her mad, we were driving her mad, my father and his sisters were driving her mad, the whole world was out to torment her. Sit down or stand up, make dinner or wash the clothes, go to sleep or stay awake. All this uncertainty was enough to drive anyone crazy.

*

My father knew what she needed if she were ever to get better. And it was not the shifting of incense urns or the digging up of hidden pots of gold. She needed to work again.

He held a special general meeting of the directors of his company. The meeting was held in our living room, and the directors were my aunties and uncles – his siblings. The meeting was to decide whether to employ my mother at the shop. My mother could not attend, and after hours of deliberation it was finally decided: my mother would start at the shop on trial.

She would start in the weeks of the school holiday break. Both my parents came to consult me. They asked if I would be able to balance my schoolwork with looking after the kids during the break, so that my ma could go to work. Would I be able to look after my siblings? For two weeks? What kind of question was that? Of course! Of course! No worries at all. I was exuberant. It was the best thing that had happened to our family for a long while. I was going to do the best job ever. I would have a working mother again, and I would spend the two weeks making the house look spick and span for when she got home. And then everything would be good again.

My mother was hired as an ordinary employee, a salesperson. She had a time card in which she had to record her hours. She was also put on the toilet-cleaning duty roster. My father brought home copies of invoices and taught her how to fill them out. "Crap, I can't do it!" she cried, because they were all in the English, and there were spaces for model numbers and serial numbers and product descriptions and all the letters and words were just scribbles and dots and where there were not scribbles and dots there were blanks. My father spent his evenings teaching her how to write "washing machine", "hair dryer" and "toaster" – a dozen times, two dozen times. She filled exercise books with the names of electrical goods, and promptly forgot them the day after. What use are five languages when you can't even fill in a simple docket for two metres of three-dollar speaker wire? "Persevere, persevere," urged my father, and told her about my second auntie from Guangzhou, who never spoke or wrote a word of English but was now working in an office in Myer. "She persisted," he told my mother. "She stuck words all over the house, even on the back of the toilet door. And your uncle grew annoyed with her, because she was always ranting in English as if she were operating a train timetable service, but still she persisted."

I watched my mother persist. She wiped down the glass counter, swept the floor, tidied up the shelves, spoke in three different languages to customers, closed sales – and then when it came time to type out and print the receipt, she was stumped. She could not follow what was on the screen, all the shapes and numbers which made words she could not understand, let alone read. She didn't know which buttons to thump. She punched in model numbers and letters, but sometimes model numbers would be difficult to locate on the computer system. In such cases, she hit the keys randomly. Sometimes receipts printed, sometimes not. When they did, and it seemed the correct amount, she was ecstatic.

When she came home, she would tell us, with pride, "I printed a receipt today." We were all very happy. I made a shopping list and my father drove me to Safeway in the evening and we bought the items. Vegetables. Pasta. Pastry. Flour. Milk. Continental Sauce. Salami. Ham. Potatoes. Tomato Paste. It was a sensible list, no junk, no nonsense food, but no Chinese food either.

Alina sat on her high chair, and I rolled out some dough for her. I rolled some for Alison too. "Play Doh!" clapped Alison.

"No, it's real food," I said. "We're going to make sausage rolls." All lunches were homemade, right down to the pizza bases and pastry dough. "You can make any shape you want," I told them, and provided an example by making a pizza shaped like a morbidly obese cat. All meals were three-course, even breakfast – a bowl of Continental Cup-a-Soup, an egg on toast and a banana and Milo.

I made up games, too. *Ice-skating with Mr Mop.* My siblings and I slid him around the entire house on the wet floors with drying cloths tied to our shoes. *Cleaning the deck of the Titanic.* A visit by Mr Mop to the back patio. *Taking down the sails.* Laundry off the line. And when they were thoroughly bored with all of this, I turned on the television, right in time for the three-o'clock kids' shows.

I would sit down at the clean granite table and spread out my schoolwork, happy in the knowledge that the house was shining. And a few hours later my mother and father would come home, and my mother would be smiling. "Wah, look how good the house looks!"

Alison would come running up with a souvenir of our day's work: "Look! Look! We made sausage rolls!" And the mood seemed to have changed somewhat, the energy in the house. My mother would even say the unnecessary – "How good!" I knew I was doing a good job, I was doing an excellent job.

But this was only for the first three days. On the fourth, my mother came home and the dark clouds had returned to her face. I braced myself for rain, for hail, for thunder. "Getting me to cut up cardboard boxes at the back!" she yelled, "what kind of job is that?" Her face did not turn red, it turned black.

"You should have said no!" My father was exasperated.

"Then what else could I have done hah? There were no customers, and I had already wiped the floors. I would be standing around like a useless person on the shop floor in front of your family! Then I would be a real joke!"

"You could have learned how to use the computers to type out invoices."

"And who is going to teach me hah? No one! Everyone is

too busy doing their own thing, or avoiding me like leprosy! And you're always in the back office. So I stand there, like a dumb idiot. What am I to do hah? I can't speak the English, and no one will teach me anything!"

My mother turned on me: "What do you think you're doing? It's time for dinner!"

Then she looked at my sisters. "And they haven't taken a shower yet! Look at them, all dirty like that!"

They had been mopping the floors, for crying out loud!

"Wah," started my father, grabbing Alina's curled little hands. "Look how red your hands are! You must be freezing!" A piece of mashed-up pie dropped to the floor.

I didn't know what was happening. Suddenly the control I had seemed to evaporate, leaving behind a raw vision of myself – I was seventeen again, and the responsibility was not mine. It was to be taken away! NO! But the house was clean, the sisters were happy, my brother had learned to bake and the school-work was still being done. What more was there to do?

On the fifth day it got better. I made sure my sisters wore their padded jackets all the time, even in the house. We made tacos. They loved tacos. "Come on, come on, let's go for a walk to 7-Eleven!" 7-Eleven was one-and-a-half kilometres away. They came back with their hands filled with Pick 'N' Mix chocolates.

My mother had the weekend off. And because she had the weekend off, so did I. I wrote in my diary, I crammed in schoolwork, I floated around the sterilised house thinking up next week's menu and plotting games. It was going to be the best holiday I ever had, the most productive. Meanwhile, my mother distractedly scrawled "Micro-Furnace Micro-Furnace

Micro-Furnace" and "Sunbeam Iron Sunbeam Iron Sunbeam Iron" in her notebooks. I could tell her heart wasn't really in it because her handwriting tumbled down the blue lines like Kamikaze pilots.

"How long do you have left of your school holidays?" she asked me.

"Oh, don't worry, a long time to go," I reassured her.

On the Monday of the second week I took my sisters to the park – yet another long walk – and to the river. We went on a mission. We went on a secret quest. We had to collect three stones along the bike path and toss them over the bridge to quell the trolls. Then we had to stand on the magical rock and ward off the evil spirits before we could progress. We had to reach for three gum-leaves to feed to the creepy-crawlies, and then walk down the hilly slopes down to the sacred Weeping Willow of the Maribyrnong River. "We did it!" cried Alina, "we did it! What do we do now, Alice?"

"The Wind in the Willow tree tells me that we get our reward."

"Yay! What is our reward?"

"A present."

"What sort of present?"

"This!"

They looked at what I proffered in my hands. "Aww, but that's just the Mars Bars we bought yesterday from 7-Eleven!"

I pressed down on them with my thumbs. "These are special Mars Bars. Feel them, they're warm." Little hands reached out for them.

"And they have been flattened by the good spirit of the Wind in the Willow tree."

"But you squashed them."

"The tree told me to."

"What's going to happen if we eat them?"

"We get new energy for our journey back. And we can carve our names on the rock!"

"Yay!"

When we returned home, as we rounded the corner to our crescent, I noticed something incongruous. Ma's car, parked in the driveway, in the afternoon. I looked at the time: 3.48 p.m. What was my mother doing home at this time? "Shh, Ma's home," I warned my sisters. They shoved their Mars Bar wrappers in their pockets. Alina's left a brown smear, but there was no time to wipe it off. I took the house keys out of my pocket and opened the door.

When I walked into the kitchen, my mother was there, just as I had feared. And she was accompanied by the black cloud.

"They gave me wrong money at the bank," she told me bluntly.

Wrong money at the bank? That was no reason to leave work early!

"What do you mean?"

"I was given wrong money to take to the bank! One hundred dollars short. I panicked. I came back to the shop. They want me gone at any cost!"

"Would you like some coffee?"

"No."

I boiled some water for Milo, for my sisters. When I had handed them their hot drinks, I sat down at the table with my mother. I didn't know what to say. Was she leaving, or was she coming back? Would she ever come back?

She started to cry. "Agheare, I can't work there any longer! I can't do it! I can't work there and I can't work at home and I can't work anywhere!"

What could I say? *Just give it another little try?* My shoulders were slumped like hers, I realised. I straightened my back. I stood up, I made her a coffee, I sat back down again. "Does Pa know about what happened?" I asked.

"Of course he does! He was there when I came back to the shop!"

"What did he say?"

"It was a mistake! He wanted to save face! Giving me $100 short to take to the bank is not a bloody mistake!"

"Maybe you should quit."

"What? And become a useless person?" she cried.

"Ma, you are not a useless person."

"I can't work and I can't not work! My mind is going crazy! I am thinking crazy thoughts."

"You are not going crazy."

"Yes, I am."

My mother would tell my father about her impending insanity when he came home from work in the evenings. My father would tell my mother that strong people did not lose their minds. "Go learn English again. Develop your skills. Take care of the kids. We have enough money for you not to work." My mother would be at this stage a raging, heaving tempest and my father would be at the end of his tether. There would be enough negative energy in that room to create a black hole on this earth, and to suck in all the sickly miasma of human failings.

*

"Mr Badger's going to go shopping tomorrow," my brother would tell my sisters in my room, making Mr Badger move on his two furry pompom excuses for feet. "What should Mr Badger buy?"

"Can we buy stuff to make pizzas?" asked Alina, sitting on the floor of my room.

"I like walking to the shops," said Alison.

I was glad to know that there were a few people in the world who still thought that walking a kilometre to the local Safeway was a great adventure. As we walked to the shops, I had a long deep think, even though I didn't want to. I had to let certain inevitabilities sink into my mind. Things were not going to be this way forever. These moments with the little ones would not last, they would grow up and lose the dimples on their fingers and the excitement of their days. Most of all, I knew these days would not last, that they were very limited, because my mother was losing the will to persist in her job.

Sure enough, even though we had worked out a perfect plan for my mother to keep working and finish at 3.30 so that she could pick the kids up after school, when the new and final term of school began, I got the flu. It was the perfect excuse. My mother stopped working for a week at the shop, and we all knew by the end of that week that it would probably be forever.

PART IV

WHEN I trudged back to Retravision after school in my blue blazer in the searing thirty-degree heat, I came across Aunt Que in the little makeshift office. The office was squashed between the Hi-Fi section and the small appliances, and had only room for a desk and a chair. Aunt Que was sitting on the chair, at the desk, and when she saw me, she sniffled. Funny that. Sniffling at work, must be hayfever, I thought, or the endless dusting of toasters. My family worked and practically lived at the shop, it was a second home, except that instead of dusting one toaster, you had to dust a dozen, and instead of watching one television after school, I could watch seven all in a row.

All our goods were kept upstairs, which meant that whenever a customer wanted anything, I had to run up and collect it for them. I would walk down with the fifteen-cup Tiger rice cooker extended in front of me as if I had got myself in a peculiar family way. In a way, I had. Our store was supposed to be a nationwide franchise, and yet our in-store price tags, labels and advertisements were usually hand-written in the dramatic-flourish brushstroke hand of my father, or filled with cheesy bug-eyed cartoons drawn by me. "Agheare, can you help me with this advertisement for the *Herald Sun*?" my father would ask me. "Agheare, does this sound right?" Letters of employment and commission were written in the upstairs of the shop, where my father and I sat at the computer crammed between television boxes and shelves of ice-crushers. We were working on a tender submission to buy a block of land from the government. My father wanted to build an electrical appliance store with a community park at the back. He had a vision of a grand utopia where electronics and the environment would be coupled in a lasting union of family fun and Saturday barbeques. I translated simple Teochew into technical business terms, and kept my teenaged self invisible on paper.

"Little Aunt, have you seen my father?" I asked. Aunt Que finally looked up at me; her eyes were rimmed red and the sniffling had not stopped. "Your father is at the hospital."

I froze. "Why?"

"Your grandmother wasn't feeling well today."

"What happened?"

She told me. I didn't understand. I made her repeat it in English. In Teochew the word sounded benign, like the careful imprint of a calligraphy brush, not the heavy finality of the English Stroke.

I had my secret places, the darkened room beneath the stairs, the attic. I went beneath the stairs, where the TDK tapes were crammed. In the darkness of the triangle-shaped enclosure, I wiped my eyes.

Granny had a stroke. I remembered the last time I saw her, in her woollen suit with the frog buttons, sitting on the edge of the double-bed we shared in Aunt Que's house in Coronation Street. The bed was double in anticipation of the nights I would sleep over. I never had rifts with my brother because I claimed Granny and her love as my own. He could have my parents, just as long as I had my grandmother and her stories and I could follow her everywhere. My grandmother was putting on her brown corduroy slip-on shoes, and I was holding her walking stick. "Come with me to buy flowers for the Buddha," she told me, and off we went to Footscray. Grandchildren were meant to be arm attachments for elderly people, like soft chattering walking frames. I held my grandmother's arm as she shuffled slowly down the street. A plastic bag floated past, and she jabbed it with her walking stick. "Cause people to trip and fall!" she muttered as we searched for the nearest bin, "Who could be so evil-hearted as to throw rubbish everywhere?" Old people, I thought, grew younger the older they became. They would see things differently, making a difference in whatever way they could, without being afraid of looking foolish. "Just accruing merit points for my next life," Granny told me, "making sure I don't turn into the dung-beetle."

Outside my alcove, I heard voices. Some Chinese lady was haggling over the price of a pre-paid phone card with one of the salespeople. "Aiyah, why not give it to me for twenty-two hah? Yes, I know twenty-five dollars is printed on the front, I am not blind, you know! But come on, I am a faithful long-time customer, give it to me for twenty-two dollars and I will take two!"

Unbelievable, I thought, but then, so many things seemed unbelievable. "Your grandmother will live forever to torment me!" my mother used to cry in the nadir of her despair, and now it was not at all certain how far forever extended. When I was ready to emerge from my dark niche, I put on a diluted customer-service smile and walked quickly back to Aunt Que's office. She was still sitting there, and she looked up at me. Her look reminded me of an old photograph I had seen of her, one of the grainy black-and-white photographs taken at the Thai refugee camp. It was a look she had attempted to eliminate ever since she arrived here, to rub out the raw peasant emotions, to be more of a market-place, marketable person. But now her mother had had a stroke, and she was stricken. For over four decades, my auntie had never been separated from her mother. Not during her youth, not during the years under Pol Pot, not even during marriage.

I stood in the doorway again. "What happened to Granny?" I needed details.

"She hadn't been feeling well for the last few days," my auntie told me. "She had headaches, and all sorts of other aches, and when she woke up this morning, she complained that she was unsteady on her feet. Then, this afternoon she fainted. Fortunately your mother was there at my house. She called me, and we sent for an ambulance."

*

Later that evening, our family went to visit my grandmother at the hospital. Everything was white and blue. The walls were white, the blankets were blue, the bed was white, the curtains were blue. And in the middle of this counterfeit cumulus-cloud-on-a-summer's-day décor, my grandmother lay in the middle of the bed, a drip extending from her arm. Her eyes were shut, but when we arrived, they slowly opened. I noticed that one eye was smaller, the eyelid seeming to have contracted.

"Your grandmother does not know she is blind in one eye," my father later whispered to me. "Don't tell her." There were many things the doctors told my parents, none of which could

172

be repeated to my grandmother. The entire left side of her body was immobilised by the stroke, and she lay in her bed, crying like a cat, tearlessly but loudly. I remembered how back in Braybrook, stray cats would come and live in our backyard and have kittens under our house. My grandmother mewed like those kittens after their mother was hit by a car, and I knew that she knew the truth no matter what the doctors and well-meaning relatives hid from her.

We placed advertisements in the weekly Chinese newspaper to find a carer. Most of the women who applied were illegal immigrants from mainland China, who worked and sent all the money home to their sons and husbands. One after another, they slept on a little fold-up bed next to my grandmother's white hospital-issued bed with the metal bars, and after a month or two, five at the most, they would leave. My grandmother was not the softest old soul to look after. She scratched, and she bit with every ounce of energy she had whenever she was being carried to the toilet. If anyone dared to try to feed her, she would yell, "Stop it! Stop it or else when I finally go, I'm going to drag you with me!" When her threats did not work, she would pick up her porcelain bowl and attempt to do grievous bodily harm to the poor soul who had dared offer help. Acupuncture doctors were brought in to try to restore movement to her legs, and she would scream her cat-being-strangled scream whenever the needles poked into her skin. She cursed those who caused her pain and cried Armageddon to them, calling forth all the ghosts she could name, and the ones she couldn't, she made up.

*

Sitting in literature class, we were discussing *King Lear*, while outside the window the gum trees tossed their heads in the grinning daylight. We spoke about life and death and God, leaving no room for my grandmother and her miscellaneous assortment of ghosts for every agonising occasion. *Paganism* was written on the board, in my teacher's sweeping handwriting. "Who can tell me what this means?" she asked.

"Belief in many gods?"

"Good. There are some cultures that still do this, aren't there?" Then she turned to me. "For example, the Chinese. They believe in and worship many Gods. Don't you, Alice?" And I did not think of my grandmother and her many gods, the chants, the plastic blue meditation mat, the swirls and whorls of the pattern on it – ten thousand shades of blue like a frenzied ocean, the smell of incense in my pores. The red-faced sword-wielding God whom we kept outside. The good-for-business God whom we called Grandfather. The Goddess of Mercy with her China-white face, her royal porcelain contentedness sitting serenely on a lotus surrounded by bald little babies, pouring water out of a vase. And the dust falling on them in the new house, because we no longer had Granny to maintain the shrine, and we no longer needed to light incense to hide the smell of baby pee rising from the carpets.

"Er, my grandmother worships many gods. Buddha, Goddess of Mercy, Lord of Business, she prays to them all to bless us." Laughter in the classroom. I didn't know whether they were laughing at my grandmother, at me or with me so I decided to laugh along, so that it would appear to be with me and not at me. I could hear Grandmother's voice in my head: "Stupid white ghosts don't understand bugger-all about real people, about the need to be protected." They were already ghosts, what need did they have of protection from ghosts? I turned back to my book, trying not to think about the strangled-cat screams and the light always left on in her room because my grandmother was afraid of the dark.

I turned back and read about King Lear going mad, mad mad, poor mad and cold old man, growing old and senile with his grotty ally Gloucester. I did not think about my grandmother diarrhoea-ing all over the floor, the mess to be cleaned up by the latest Shanghai carer who we declared as our "cousin" to health authorities because secrets should never be told. "Oh, the madness, the passion, the pain, the poignancy of *King Lear*, this is life, this is distilled emotion!" cried my Literature teacher. "Oh, the beauty and horror." So in essays I wrote about the beauty and the horror, and the madness and the glory. I did not think of the madness of my grandmother, whose mind was still so sharp but who could only stare at the ceiling and wait for my auntie to arrive home from work. None of that seemed real. The only sort of real that had any meaning and depth was depicted in the white and black pages of Shakespeare, the universality of human experience accessible only to erudite people who could read it. We were living a new life now, there was no room in my head for death and disease and illness.

But whenever I went to visit my grandmother, the old world would come flooding back. "Agheare," she would coax from the bed, "are you cold? Oh, your hands, so cold!" She would grab my hand in hers and fill my ears with words that made perfect sense to her – visions of her young girlhood self who cried for her mother back in Chaozhou, China. But in my other hand, I would be holding my opened book, and I would be hearing one thing and seeing another, until nothing made much sense to me anymore.

I WOKE up one morning with a false skin on my face. This skin was made of rubber, and it took great effort to move the muscles. I put my fingers on either side of my face and pinched, but no red came, not even patchy fingermarks. I could not prise off this rubber death-mask. I felt a funeral in my brain, and we hadn't even studied Emily Dickinson yet.

I was seventeen, and all the right things seemed to happen to me at the right time. I had got into a good school. I got the usual Asian High-Achiever marks. I had even been asked out by a boy. But the "right" things, like everything else in my life, had their false, unsettling undertones. In the good school I existed slumped against walls and slinking through corridors. And the Sunshine boy who asked me out told me that he had put a gun to someone's head at fifteen because he was so angry that his mate was *chasin'*. I would go to the grammar school and watch the clean bad boys downloading angry rap lyrics about the same "issues" over the internet, because life here *was not a life, man*. "*This* is life, man, this is da life." That *was* da life, and they were lucky that they only had to live it vicariously.

They thought that I was the naive girl, the one in the ivory tower of books and ideas, nothing running down my skin except soap and detergent suds. Who did not know what "da life" was, who lived in a big bubble, or a zillion little bubbles soft and white. With one red steaming hand in the sink I could smother them all without a sound, and run the knife under the water, all the while reading *The Age of Innocence*. And I too, could forget the reality of this life, believing that my real life would begin sometime soon.

When this false one ended.

*

No one noticed the rubber mask until it started to leak. After a month, my mother could not stand it, so she took me to the doctor. "Tell Dr Cheng everything," she commanded. "Everything that is wrong."

In the car, I imagined the consultation. What is wrong, Alice? *Everything.* There. *Tah-Dah!* The end. Curtains for me, please, or perhaps a white sheet.

But when I arrived and he asked me the question, nothing would come out.

I wiped my nose with my sleeve. It was getting incredibly difficult to find dry areas along my wrist.

Our good doctor passed the box of tissues towards me. Then he held out a pen and pad. Printed on the top of the page was a medical company's name and, beside that, a flaming-torch logo which looked more like the tentacles of death. Below were dotted pale grey lines

"Then write," he commanded in English. My mother was right next to me watching. I took hold of the pad and the pen.

"Go on, write down what is wrong for the doctor," she urged.

How could I do this? I looked down at the pad. I held the

pen in my other hand. I made a little dot on the paper. There. A speck. Done.

I handed Dr Cheng back his pad.

"What's this?" he asked.

"Don't know."

He looked at my mother. My mother looked at him, eyes as wide as soup bowls.

"What does this mean, Doctor?" she asked. She pointed to my speck.

I'll tell you what it means, I wanted to say, *It means I am going dotty.*

"Doesn't mean anything," said the doctor, "unless Alice says it means something."

"Then what do we do?"

He wrote slowly on a piece of paper with great concentration.

"Here. Take this. It's the name and number of a very good specialist."

"You mean a mind-doctor?"

"Yes."

"But why does she need a mind-doctor?"

I didn't know myself, but Dr Lim's office was pale, with pastel-coloured walls, and it smelled nice – there was a big bouquet of flowers bursting from the brim of the vase on the bench. Inner-city address, best Asian-Australian shrink in town, though we Indochinese usually didn't usually go to shrinks, we prayed to the Lord Buddha for good obedient kids. *But what happens when you get them exactly as you prayed for? When they cannot cope when there are no more orders to follow? When there are no consistent orders to follow?* I looked at the flowers – tulips allegedly made Sylvia Plath better, but these weren't doing much for me.

It was hard to focus on what grey-suited, square-glassed Doctor said to me in our hour, and most of it didn't make sense because he was talking about athletes. "Alice, you know those Olympic runners always wanting to win?" he said, the weight of two degrees behind his back in solid silver frames, "always striving for number one? They like to believe that they will always be number one, and they train hard for it. But the reality, we know, is that some day some other person is going to beat them and be number one."

I couldn't have cared less about numbers. Cipher was not a number. But my mother and father nodded in agreement – number ones, number eighty-eights, number fours. They understood. Four sounded like the word for "dead" in Chinese, so if you were Cantonese you could never use that word. *Sei lah! Sei Sei Sei*! Dead dead dead dead. My grandmother never let us use the word because she was scared of dead, and death, and the dead. But if we were all going to die anyhow, why not live life, why not even wag school?

Soon there were more meetings, this time with the school administration, and I found myself sitting in the vice-principal's office with my anxious fingers tearing holes in my blazer pockets and a smile fixed on a face that was no longer mine. This time the staff did not tell me, as they had before, "You should apply for university scholarships, Alice, you'll surely get them."

But the smile still stayed in place.

The vice-principal looked into my eyes. She had clearly seen this many times before, and could probably count herself to sleep by listing the nervous breakdowns she had dealt with in her office.

"What pills have the doctors prescribed for you, Alice?"

There were little pink pills to help me focus, big white ones to help me settle, tiny white ones to help me sleep. And not only were there pills, there were natural therapies. Horlicks and bananas. Incense and charms. And the depths of my pa's medicine pot always contained boiled black monstrosities which came in white paper packages from the Barkly Street apothecary.

Before I went to sleep each evening, my father came in with his electronic acupuncture machine. He attached the pods of his acupuncture device to my tummy, to my calves. "Got this in Singapore," he told me, "Lucky hah? It doesn't hurt like the needles do." Pim pim pim pim pim went the little electric pin-pricks.

He massaged my neck, my shoulders, my feet. When he tickled me on the soles of my feet, I did not move. I had stopped feeling ticklish ever since this shadow began stalking me. It was scary being stalked. What could this dark shadow do to a person? It had already made my feet feel black and gangrenous. They looked like my grandmother's wasted toes, with her crusty toenails like dirty broken brown shells dropping off on the sheets.

"Don't be ridiculous, don't know where you come up with this crazy stuff," scolded my mother. "Your feet look fine."

She looked down and saw long, evenly coloured toes. Skin the colour of washed sand against my father's gnarled old tree-twig fingers. She did not see the gangrene. She did not see the leprosy, she could not tell that I was wasting away. Or perhaps she did not want to see it. "You are fine," they all told me. My body was still working, my brain cells were still intact, I was *not* going mad mad mad.

"Pa, go to sleep. I'll be okay," I said.

Pa did not believe me.

"Did you take your pills?"

"Yes." My hand wrapped around the soggy solid spots in my pocket.

"Even the pink ones?"

"Yes."

"Don't lie," said my mother, standing over me. "We haven't even given you those yet." I lay there, blinking up at the ceiling.

"Why don't you take it?"

Smaller than a Smartie, it nestled under my tongue. I hoped it was not getting comfortable and ready to multiply. I swallowed.

"Did you take it?"

I opened my mouth, poked out my tongue.

"Good."

No, it was not good. It was awful. It felt like crushed cyanide powder beneath my tongue. Specks floated on top, to the area where you taste bitterness. *Now I feel like an authentic Chinese woman*, I thought. *Yippee, adolescence is over! I'm all better now.*

"Now go to bed."

I got up from the bed, went to one of our four toilets, closed the door and spat it into the bowl. *Bye bye, bitter pill. Parting is such sweet sorrow.* Down it swirled. *Bye bye, clouds of clarity.* I would rather be blocked than have this false sense of calm. Back to the room I went, back to bed. Between the sheets I slipped, and no longer did I write in my journal. There weren't even any anxious etchings anymore. I had no words left.

"Go to bed," said my mother, "go to sleep."

Can't, I wanted to tell her, there's a hole in my solar plexus. I think I can put my hand through it, and if I reach deep enough and high enough, I can also feel my chest cavity – black, miasmic and sick. I'm leaking to death, and if I should die before I wake, I pray my organs the donor registry to take.

But who would want this sick mind? How I would have loved to reach in there, twiddle with a few wires, tweak a few neurons and electrons, and bring me back to life.

*F*OR my valedictory dinner, my mother bought me a white dress, because she thought it would make me happier. I wondered whether she could see that it would also be like dressing a body for a polished pine box. At my house, my friend Nina took one look at the scalloped lace and told me she would lend me one of her frocks. She insisted that I come to her house after school the next day, so I did. Volition had disappeared altogether from me. If someone had told me to lie in the pine box in the white gown with the neat lace shells tumbling down my arms and knees, I would have obliged. If they had closed the lid, I would have gone to sleep. I was in that semi-asleep state when Nina told me to turn around so she could see the sleeveless cheongsam she had put on me. It fitted like a black skin with a rash of orange and green blossoms. "You look good in that," she said, adjusting the collar.

When Nina and her mother came by on the afternoon of the dinner to take me to the hairdresser, my mother was in bed staring at something – her hands, the light, the wall. Something. Beneath my coat, I wore the borrowed black dress. I preferred its fermenting scent of perfumed secondhand sweat to the cold sterility of a forced innocence. "I am leaving now," I called out to my mother in her room.

"What are you wearing?" she yelled downstairs, without getting up from the bed.

Defeated, I could not lie.

As I finally got into my friend's car, I was as clumsy as a doll dressed by a child four decades old. I was a wind-up obedience toy, or a coathanger for good intentions gone awry. I was almost eighteen.

"Look at her shoes." Nina pointed them out to her mother as we waited at the hairdresser.

"My goodness, look at your shoes." Nina's mother shook her head with a sad smile. On my feet were shiny plastic middle-aged-woman pumps, yellowy-silver off-white. "These white shoes match the dress," my mother had said.

"Don't worry, you can come back to my house and borrow a pair of mine," Nina reassured me. Again I was back at her house, and this time I sat on the edge of the spa bath and looked down at a pair of white stilettos, with lots of thin white straps at the ankles. Nina had made my feet look like party feet, like feet that danced to synthesised tunes and rubbed against young men. I was grateful to Nina. She had taken me to her parent's ensuite bathroom and put her mother's expensive perfume on my wrists. She had prodded and poked me into perfection. She was even diplomatic enough not to have said anything in the car as I handed back the black dress in a plastic bag.

"You should pluck your eyebrows," she told me. I didn't want to. I liked my eyebrows, black and thick like the Indian ink I used when I was eight and took Chinese brush painting lessons. She got out the tweezers for me, and I yanked out a few hairs to make her happy. I sat on the edge of Nina's spa-tub, watching her smear herself all over with a cream the colour of caramel, looked down at my party feet and waited for our parents to pick us up.

"Look at you. So lovely." The comments meant nothing to me that evening. I was carrying an empty shell around that did not belong to me, positioning it in different unobtrusive places in the grand function room, the girl with the rubber mask of a face.

We were on the only fully "ethnically-enhanced" table: Neylan's mother in her jilbab, Natalia's generous gregarious Russian parents, and Nina's glamorous Vietnamese parents. Natalia's aside, these were the parents who did not know much English, who drove taxis and sewed collars and buttons by the boxful so that they could send their children to a school such as this and watch them mingling with the upper echelons of society – the children of lawyers and doctors and professionals.

That night our parents realised something that probably shook them from their sleeping dream, the semi-dazed dream they entered when they rested from too many taxi-shifts, or when they closed their eyes from the fatigue of opening too many stitched buttonholes. They realised that their children were Watchers, just as they were. We watched everyone else, as tonight we watched our classmates in their smart suits and sophisticated frocks climb onto the stage to pose for photographs.

"Why don't you get on stage too?" my parents asked me. As if I could just jump on stage with people I had never spoken three words to all year and insert myself gracefully into their picture. And suddenly the reality must have sunk in for my parents, for *all* the parents on our table, that their children were not more popular, that we did not talk to the beautiful people. It must have hit them hard – that we were still sticking by each other, sticking with each other, and not getting out, not fitting in. They had thought of this new life in simple cause-and-effect terms: that if they worked their backs off to send their children to the grammar school, then we would automatically mingle with the brightest and fairest of the state.

But to the beautiful ones, we were the non-party people, the ones with frightening parents and skirts down to our ankles. To the intellectual ones, we were the ones who never had enough time to join in debating, the boring compliant people who just studied and studied. If only they knew our lives did not revolve around study as much as theirs did – but they would never know. We may have been the dull people with no time, privacy or glamour, but we had our fierce pride.

With my camera, I migrated to my older teachers, the sanest people in the whole royal red and gold room full of colour like a watermelon turned inside out, soft and pastel and pink in some places and yet sharp and blood-red in others. The future people would get their photographs developed from this evening and see the yesterday girl, the small one standing next to them, the one wearing the funny twelve-year-old bridesmaid's dress, and five years down the track they would not remember her name.

I had nothing to lose. So I walked up to Edmund Chan-Johnson, tall awkward Edmund with the serious brown eyes who had no idea that he had been loved all year by the silent girl sitting two seats behind him in Literature class.

"Edmund."

He saw me. He said the words I had him rehearse in my

mind a million times so that when it really happened I would be gracious and generous. But I had heard it from and told it to so many others so many times this evening that they didn't mean anything. *Don't lie, Edmund*, I thought, *my lipstick is too dark, my shoes are too high and I look like Lolita going to confirmation. I don't look like the real me, I have never looked like me and you have never ever looked at me.* But instead I muttered, "You look good too."

"Thanks."

"Can I have a picture with you?"

"Umm, sure."

After Nina took the photo, I ran away with my camera flailing at my side.

She caught up with me and we returned to our table, to take the *real* photographs, photographs of the people who mattered most to us – our parents and friends.

And then it was all over, and I was back home in the bathroom pulling the black bobby pins from my hair and wiping the make-up from my face with cotton balls, pulling off the white dress and getting into mismatched pyjamas, lying in bed waiting for the long sleep to come.

*

By the time my exams arrived, I was so far gone that even reading the newspaper was difficult. Suddenly, all writing confounded me. Sentences suffocated me, they seemed strung together like code. "It's only some stupid exams," my parents told me. "Just aim to pass. A pass is all you need." They were not even convincing themselves. They knew that in my condition I would not be able to live a normal life, let alone sit exams.

At school I was sent to a little office I had never known existed. There Mrs Trengrove taught me how to breathe. How many other people visited this office, I wondered. How many of our smiley-faced classmates came every Wednesday, every Tuesday to learn how to breathe? "You're not going to fail," the counsellors all told me.

You don't understand, I wanted to say. If I fail, I am condemned to a life sentence of dirty dishes and rubber-faced, blank-wall staring, and I will go mad. If I fail, everything my whole life was meant to lead up to will be gone. "Study hard and go to university," my grandmother had always told me, my grandmother who now lay staring at the ceiling in a dark and musty room. "Study hard and be a scholar." Failure was annihilation. I was never the spunky valedictorian girl declaring her smartness to the world with a defiantly upturned chin, I was the one slinking into shadows with my eyes glued to my books hoping only to fulfil the set criteria. I was a blank just like the walls with the posters removed. How easily they came off – they were only stuck on with blu-tack, like my personality.

My Auntie Ly visited Cambodia and came back with stories about our impoverished, skinny cousins – all in their late forties, all unmarried. "Please, Ly," they begged her, "please set us up with men in Australia so we can get out." They had waited too long to marry, they had waited for men who could take them abroad. They did not want to settle for a local, because they did not want to settle for a life in Cambodia. My auntie promised that she would do her best to help them look, but said, "I don't know many men, the ones I know are divorced or wife-bashers." "I don't care, I don't care!" the cousins insisted. They just wanted to get out.

I understood them, these poor cousins. I understood how terribly they must have ached to get out. My role now, after final exams and the end of high school, was to wait for my hair to grow and then attach my tentacles to an emotionally un-bruised boy with a doctor's bag. It wouldn't be too hard to do – I was in high demand with demanding mothers-in-law, and eventually one of them was bound to have a son doing medi-cine. Then I would be his little attachment, and I would not have to say a word. There would be a courtship by half-smiles and lowered lashes, crossed legs and charming blunders. She can cook a good bowl of rice. She is parsimonious, it is guaran-teed by her mother. A lifetime warranty. At least I could marry well.

I felt great contempt for anyone who was interested in me at this time. I thought they were sick, to want something so sick. The horror of it all was that they liked me *as I was*. How could they love this *me*, sapped of all essence? They loved a shell, they were content with a shell. This was what my future held – I was a void to be filled by others.

I had done everything right, and I had turned out so wrong. I turned out empty. I turned out faulty. I felt like my grand-mother, lying in bed staring up at the ceiling, waiting for it all to end, yet so afraid of the end that she always slept with a light on. "Agheare," she cried, "take me to a place with no darkness." Oh Grandmother, if we could both go to a place with no dark-ness, I would get us first-class tickets edged with gold. You can chant your Amitabhas and I'll have red ribbons in my hair, and my little hand will fit in yours as perfectly as it did when I was small, and I will not demand that you buy me anything along the way, and you can wear your pink lipstick because you would never go out without your lipstick. Oh Grandma, wherever we go and whomever you meet along the way, you will tell them, "This is my granddaughter, she is so clever, she is so smart. She knows everything, for someone so young. Aiia, she can also make anything and do everything."

"*H*EY Alice, Granny died."

"When?" I put down my bags. It was the last thing I expected to hear from my little sister Alison.

"Last night."

My grandmother had caught a cold, my father explained, her immune system was down. It happened in the middle of the night, he told me, it happened so quickly that by the time he drove to Aunt Que's house my grandmother was gone. That was all my parents would tell me. They probably wanted to spare me the details. I had been away for a few days on a camp, and they could not bring themselves to break the news to me in the car driving home.

"Oh no," was all I could say. My grandmother was not meant to die. She was meant to be with me forever. Even in her illness she was the one person who was always happy to see me, and she did not care that my store of Teochew words was diminishing. She knew we were both going the way of the ghosts, except my ghosts were white living ones and hers were unknown. "The Buddhas will protect us," she told me, "just pray to them in times of darkness, and there will be light."

My grandmother's funeral lasted for three days and three evenings, with people from the Bright Moon Buddhist Association chanting prayers around the clock. Granny who used to set me on the table, was now laid out on a table herself, dressed in imperial yellow with a little yellow cap. During the last stage of her illness her white hair had started to grow back black, as if miraculously there was renewed life, as if her body were regenerating, a reincarnation without death. But now all this regrowth was covered by the cap, and when I looked at her I knew that something vital had slipped out, so all that was left was the shell of a person.

My grandmother was meant to be a part of me forever, so that I would always know that there was a life before me, and a life after me. My grandmother and her stories. What would I do without them? She asserted my existence before I knew I had one – before I was conscious I had a life beyond the present – and she told me my childhood. "Agheare, when you were small you could recite long Teochew songs and poems." "Agheare, when you were small you could speak in Cantonese." It seemed as if I could do anything when I was small. We slept in the same bed, and it was always warm. Now there would be no one left to remind me of my roots, no one to tell me to be proud to be part of a thousand-year-old culture, no one to tell me that I was gold not yellow.

During a break in the ceremony and chanting, I looked over at my mother and noticed that one of her arms was heavily bandaged. "What happened to your arm, Ma?"

"When you were at camp, the soldering torch I was using slipped," she explained. The instrument she was using for her jewellery work was so old that it had burst into flames and given her third-degree burns.

"The job is dangerous," my father told me, "so your mum is not going to be doing it anymore." She was going to sell all her machines and take her framed *Registration of Business* down from the wall of our house.

So the day my grandmother died was also the day my mother finally decided to end her outworking career. It was a decision resulting from an accident – but the decision itself was no accident, it was one we had seen coming for a long time. I didn't suppose my mother knew what she was going to do with her time now, but she had made the decision at last and I figured she would find something. After all, time was so finite, it was the only thing you couldn't buy. "You can't buy old people," my grandmother had told me the last time I visited her, "you can hand over some money and buy a little child, but you can't buy old people. So remember, Agheare, to spend your time well with your parents." Then I remembered another thing she said to me, punctuated with the deepest saddest sigh her old lungs could exhale: "But who would want to buy a useless old person like me anyway?"

EVERY year for the past five years I had made a list of "fifty things to do before I die". I now needed a new list every day, a list I would lose and forget, a list that told me to wake up and get out of bed and eat and walk and move and smile and bathe. This was my list.

Yet the exams came and went, and I sat them.

"Now your exams are over, you can go out and play," my mother told me. "Go on, go and have fun while you're young. Go out with boyfriends." If I was in a normal state of mind, I would have keeled over and died of shock.

"Brush your hair in the mornings," my father urged. "Make yourself look pretty."

"Do some housework, that will keep your mind off things," my mother advised me. "This is all your fault," she would rail at my father. "See, you have spoilt her. Now she can't even do housework, doesn't even want to crawl out of bed in the morning."

I could not muster the energy to see friends or to look presentable. When friends asked me out after final exams, I would tell them yes, yes over the phone. But immediately after hanging up, the anxieties would start to kick in. Oh no, I could not do it. I could not appear in public. They would be able to see through this rubber mask. They would know how unwell I was, and they would never see me in the same way again.

After much coaxing from my parents, and after I had taken on a deathly pallor, I agreed one day to go bowling for a distant friend's birthday. My parents were so glad that my mother even drove me to Highpoint shopping complex and gave me forty dollars.

When I arrived, there were so many people. So many people in the mall, all scurrying to buy things or try things or keep their eye on things, and I wondered, was that all there was to life? During the whole ordeal, all I could do was smile. I smiled the way a skull smiles, all teeth and no flesh. It was eerie to my friends, this rictus of someone who was feigning that they were still alive when in actuality the shell had been cracked and the person inside had escaped.

I rolled one weak ball after the other down the alley. I used the lightest balls, but they felt as if they were ripping my arm off. So much energy to lift them and then drop them, and what was the point of all this?

Everyone pretended that there was nothing wrong with me, all playing along with my deceit. They didn't know what else they could do, with a friend who had helped them with their assignments and edited their English pieces, who had counselled them through boyfriends and been the excuse for them to see their lovers.

I rarely went out after that. To friends who didn't know about my condition, I wrote letters, each convivial sentence forced out like a self-inflicted punishment. There was only one friend, Kathryn, who could actually stand my company. Once she gave me a yellow gerbera and spent a day trying to cheer me up. She took me out to lunch and we went to the beach. I couldn't believe that she could tolerate my presence, this big gaping hole beside her. She stayed on the phone with me despite the silences on my side because I had no more words to give. She talked to me as she was taking her dog for a walk, and invited me to her house where she played the violin for me. She was Goodness Incarnate, but I still felt the summer stretch ahead like a rope, a rope for a head that was now defunct.

I couldn't imagine working at Retravision anymore. All the staff and all the customers would find out. Here is the Manager's daughter, the one who couldn't get into university. All that money, all that waste. "Don't tell people how you are, don't show your aunties how you are at the moment," my parents commanded me.

I sat in my room wiping my eyes and nose with tissues, because I didn't even have the energy or courage to read. Reading alarmed me, it confused me even more. I was frightened every time I came across a sentence that I was meant to understand but couldn't. Eventually, this became every sentence I read. I would invariably compare my life to the words and feel deep in my belly that I was doing it all wrong. Nothing I read assured me that anything I did was right. People became blurs. The walls became my only constant companion, so white and pristine, and solid, but I knew they were just plasterboard, and that one heavy blow would reveal the hollowness inside, and the wooden skeleton of the house. I sat and slept in the same place, I spent days and weeks in the same spot. I no longer slept in my bed, but spread my blankets on the little space of floor between the bed and the wall, like a gap between cliffs into which I had fallen.

One day Alina came in.

"Hello little one," I said. "Come here. Come here to me."

She was in the green tracksuit of her school uniform, with the bowl haircut that I had given her. She came and sat in my lap. I put my arms around her, comforted by her familiar and strange musty smell of digging up insects during recess and relocating them to different parts of the turf.

"You are a champ," I told her.

We sat in silence for a while. Then I heard her sniffling.

I could not believe it.

All my sadness was rubbing off onto her. It was contagious, this disease. I didn't know what to do.

I decided there had to be an end to this. The next day I decided to do something useful. I decided to clean out the cutlery drawer. *It doesn't mean anything*, the crowd in my head told me, *Nothing means anything. Why are you even doing this?*

Shut up, I said inside my brain, shut up. At least I am doing something.

But it means nothing.

Even if it means nothing, I am at least doing something.

Nothing means anything.

Shut up, I can't hear you. La la la.

It's all a waste of time.

I am picking up a fork now. The fork goes in this plastic compartment with the other forks. I knew it was all drivel, but I had to keep talking to myself to stifle the voices. Now I have a spoon in my hands. Where do you go, spoon? With all the other spoons over here …

You're going to live out the rest of your life doing things that don't mean anything.

And now five chopsticks. Where is the sixth? Oh, there you are.

And then you're going to die.

But I was still here when Judgment Day arrived. The results were to be released on Monday by post, but friends were calling up the hotline to find out their results early. Ninety-three, ninety-four, ninety-five. Incredible-sounding numbers, a thousand doors opening up to them. Just like the ancient imperial civil service examinations in China, which any poor villager could sit and so become eminent. With a 1200-year history of examinations behind us, who could blame us for being obsessed with tests? My grandmother had tried to tell me all these things, but my Chinese ears were not Chinese enough to pick up the sounds and meanings of her words. I had grown too old for Granny's "in the past" stories. But I needed them now. Oh Granny, what did they do in the past when they failed exams? In the past, women couldn't even take exams. I should consider myself lucky.

My parents wanted me to call up the hotline too. They told me that it would put an end to my torment, but I think they meant "our" torment – our collective torment. So I dialled the number and listened for the automatic voice prompts. After I punched in my student number, I waited to hear my final marks.

I hung up immediately.

I must have heard wrong. I gave a loud yowl. What a terrible joke. Someone up there really had it in for me.

My parents ran into the room, worried that I had leapt out of the upstairs window. All they saw was me with the cordless phone in my hand, looking at it.

I told them what I had heard over the phone.

I told them I must have heard wrong.

My father told me to dial again. I did.

I had not heard wrong the first time.

"You got your results now, you don't need to be anxious anymore," my mother told me.

How did it happen, I wondered. I was so drugged on the day of my English exam that I didn't know what I was writing. I almost missed my Literature exam because I had drifted into on-off sleep on the couch. As for the other subjects, well, I didn't even want to go there. Maybe there were parts of my brain that retained all the information, even though I thought I had lost it all like a virus-ridden computer that had crashed.

"You got into law at Melbourne University!"

"You got a scholarship from Monash University!"

"You got an award from the Minister of Education!"

I got out. I had got out. I was no longer stuck. Time to rub the circulation back into the ankles, time to get those forms in quickly, to make sure I was enrolled so that I could introduce myself at parties as "Alice, Arts/Law, hey how about you?" All was well, all stereotypes were fulfilled and everything was in its proper place. Onwards towards the Great Australian Dream. You can pass go. You can collect $2000. You will be going to university.

The crowd in my head did not give me any applause, they just eventually scattered. But they scattered slowly, painfully slowly, like an irascible old person leaving a good seat at the theatre. It took months for all of the scattered thoughts to disappear. They were like vampires, needing my blood and energy to sustain them for that just one more day, that one more hour. But I would move on, move away, move up. They would *die*, and I would live.

*T*HAT summer, before university started, I worked as a salesgirl at the shop and was put in charge of the mobile-phone counter. I realised that I always retreated to this place after something traumatic had happened. Who needs a mental hospital in which to recover when you have a landmark store smack-bang in the middle of Footscray? Post-nervous break-down or feeling like a wreck? Nothing that a few extremely aggro hagglers won't fix up. They'll jolt you out of your torpor: "Whaddya mean this is two years outa warranty eh? I want me money back. Youse power points are shifty!"

To connect a mobile phone took at least half an hour. There were forms to fill and covers to choose. Then there was the call to Telstra for the credit check and connection. I could sense customers becoming impatient, particularly when it was their first time and they didn't realise how long it would take. To keep them from going across the road, I would sit them down, make them instant Nescafé. I thought that mastering the art of small talk was difficult enough, but then there was also the Big Talk. I was not prepared for the Big Talk, or the desperate need for it, the sheer human necessity for a witness to a life of loneliness and misery. I met Mrs Christian, a beautiful but bleary-eyed Filipino woman in her early forties, who needed me to connect her to a mobile phone because her husband kept beating her up and bringing his mates home to "do" her. When the Telstra woman told me over the phone that Mrs Christian would not be connected because she lacked a permanent address and credit history, I didn't know what to tell her. "Dey not going to connect me, I know." She knew already, like all those used to an unbroken history of bad news. She knew the price you paid for wanting to leave your family to go to a country where you lost all your connections, so that there was no older brother to beat up your abusive husband.

Old women would pat my hand – "Don't be so anxious dear, I'm not in a hurry" – and tell me that they weren't even allowed to see their grandkids, let alone buy them DVD players for Christmas. "Your culture, dear, now you've got it right, you look after your elders."

And then there was Miss Beauty Queen Emilia, who frequently visited but rarely bought anything. She wore rubber gloves soiled with garden dirt, tracksuit pants and a glittery blazer. "Can't buy anything today," she would say, "only have fifteen cents." And she would open up her coin purse to show me. Whenever she did buy something, she would get me to type her name on the receipt as "Miss Beauty Queen Emilia", because that was what she claimed she had been back in Cambodia. And there was the blind Vietnamese man in the blue *Wedding-Singer*-like blazer, who, like Miss Beauty Queen Emilia, would also not buy anything but would want a female salesperson to walk him through the entire store. He clutched our arms so tightly that we were afraid we'd be amputees by the end of the round, but we humoured him for many months, until my uncle decided to be the escort one day. After that, the blind man was not too sure about his tours anymore, and would want to hear our voices as well. Or there was the man in the motorised wheelchair who dressed in a leopard-print cloak like a sedentary Tarzan, who bought speaker-wire every fortnight for some obscure purpose, and the director of the funeral parlour down the road, who bought an inexplicable number of blank video-tapes every week.

My mother brought my father and me homemade three-course meals for lunch – roast pork, rice noodles, bitter gourd soup, banana-tapioca pudding. She spent the remainder of her time driving my sisters to school and picking them up, and in between she sat with us in the lunch-room during our lunch-breaks. The lunch-room was the place where all the idle scuttle-butting went on, about difficult customers we'd had that day and customers who were building new houses in Caroline Springs or Sydenham. My aunties and mother would have yelling sessions about how they saw this or that woman and how they were now aging like a dried longan, and call it a good conversation. Meanwhile, the non-Chinese employees would huddle over the *Herald Sun*, quietly scoff down their pizza or take-away fried rice and get the hell out of there as fast as possible, since they had no idea whether our yelling was about them or not.

*

Those innocent aunts who had started off living in the housing commission flats were now married and also working in the family business, and Aunt Sim was due to have her first baby. I remembered when Aunt Sim first arrived from Vietnam – she was fifteen and she clutched a new boxed doll in her hand, probably the only doll she had ever owned, but she willingly, smilingly handed it to me, an already spoilt-rotten Australian kid with too many toys. Aunt Sim did the work of four people at our other shop in Springvale. Not only was she a salesperson, she also did the accounts, office administration and stock orders and she did it all in such a gentle and efficient manner that after a while it was easy to forget the miracle of how she managed so much. When she went on maternity leave, my father did not know what to do.

Then a surprising thing happened. Over dinner, my mother announced, "I'm going to go and help out in the store." She looked at my father. "You know, just to keep a lookout and watch to see that there are no shoplifters."

We were stunned.

"What a good idea."

"Mind you, just while my sister goes off and has her baby."

"Yes, you would be of so much help since we are so short of staff."

"Might as well go help out the family business," she said.

So that was how my mother decided to go back out into the world again.

She did not buy new clothes for work. She wore her old clothes and no make-up, and she used the same tactics to sell as she used to bargain at the market in Footscray. She had suddenly caught on to the way the market-place operated, and realised that she did not need to know the technical specifications of a widescreen plasma television to sell one. All that mattered was that the price was right. And she was a master at haggling. The same skills she had used with the Kims she now brought to our franchise. Springvale had the biggest Chinese-Cambodian community in Victoria, and my mother seemed to know the art of selling better than we who had been educated here, we who were sent to expensive corporate training workshops in the Head Office.

She was not relying on us so much to translate the English. She was picking it up, very slowly. I wrote out step-by-step pictorial instructions, on a little sheet for her to keep in her pocket, on how to type up a receipt. And we discovered an extraordinary thing: that customers tended to trust this forty-something housewife more than a trained salesperson. My mother was bent on not letting customers walk out of the store. "Ay! Ay!" she would call from halfway across the store, "Sir! Ma'am! Come back! Come back and I will do better one for you, I promise." Sometimes she even *dragged* the Asian customers back into the shop. To ordinary Australians that would be harassment, but to Southeast Asians it was a convincing sale, it meant that the seller wanted your business so much they were willing to chase you down the street to give you a good deal.

My mother could identify with the new migrants, even those from far-off countries like Sudan and Ethiopia. She knew what kind of products they would ask for, and she knew they would be comfortable bargaining. *She* knew how to say the numbers in English, *they* knew how to say the numbers in English, and so a deal was struck. She knew that they had to carry their goods home on the train or bus, so she secured them extra tightly with pink twine.

Soon she became one of the top salespeople in Springvale, and there was nothing she could not sell. She did better than us with our English and youth and white-ghost ways. "I sold three microwaves and a fridge today," she would tell us after work, and we would wahhhh, wishing we too could sell three microwaves and a fridge in one day. Sometimes she would work in Footscray too, or I would go to Springvale, and there was a certain kind of affinity one felt when working alongside one's parents.

My father never wore a suit to work – he always wore his maroon jumper, with the little Retravision logo stitched to one side. Over that he wore his tattered brown leather jacket. The customers felt sorry for him, this skinny man in the brown jacket with the perseverance of Gandhi, trying his best to sell a fridge twice his size.

My father had built all this up from scratch, and it never ceased to amaze him. He was never meant to be a franchise-holder with this company. When he set up business selling watches and singing Christmas cards, there was already a Retravision in Footscray, but still he made his submission to the Board of Directors. They refused him again and again until he finally convinced them to give him the franchise licence because he could corner the new Asian-immigrant market. My father made his business success in the same way he made toys for us. In a world of finite time and resources, my father still found time to make toys when we were small, and you could break those toys ten thousand times and yet they would remain unbroken because there was always another egg roly-poly to make, another wax dripping earring to cast. "You can make a better one," he would urge us.

Before he started his electronics business, my father ate three sandwiches a day while working at the Alcan factory by day and studying goldsmithing at RMIT by night. He would sit outside the lawns of the State Library with his last sandwich, watching the darkness, and think of glories to come.

On my birthday, my mother brought a cake into the store. She took it to the front counter, and lit the candles, while all the sales staff sang happy birthday to me. Customers joined in, and we served the cake around. I felt a flush of mortification and joy, and the strangest ineffable feeling of pride and place, even though the place was just a spot in behind the mobile-phone counter. For now I was just a salesgirl in a blue sales shirt and red lipstick, but I was special. The cake proved it. It blared out this message, accompanied by the backing vocals of a special durian scent, so that no one within a fifteen-metre radius could miss it.

University would soon begin, but this here and now was my life, my Garden of Eden littered with loud bangs and hilarious street signs pointing to places with a possibility of salmonella. This was where it all happened for me, where my life was lived. Here there were people who appreciated my skills and who brought me three-course lunches and cakes for my birthday, strangers who would clap for me and women who would confide to me all their home problems. Lonely old men from the Barkly Hotel across the road with brown-paper bags and marriage proposals. Here were the blind, the lame, the wordless, the mindless, the mute, all briefly passing in through the doors for their cameo appearances, and then leaving again. Here I was just nobody, really; nobody distinctive, nobody important. But here I was somebody loved for being precisely that. Life was finally beginning to feel stable.

PART V

"AH BuKien wants to discuss Agheare for her son," my mother announced to my father over breakfast one morning. They spoke as if I wasn't there, but they expected me to eavesdrop. This woman, a family friend of my parents, had been intent on seeing me marry her son ever since she had laid eyes on me that morning as a shapeless pre-pubescent in my mother's hand-me-downs. Ha, the absurdity of it. "That crazy antiquated relic thinks she's still living in Confucian times," my father scoffed. "She doesn't realise that in this modern era parents don't arrange their children's hearts for them."

Oh, I remembered the woman well. Once, she had come over to our house to comment on my nose. Another time, we went to her double-storey house in the centre of Footscray – the house she built from selling rice noodles. Every time my parents drove past that colossal mansion sitting smug between the dilapidated Victorian dwellings, they would point out the window and say, "Look, there's BuKien's rice-noodle house." The day my parents decided to visit, I knew that it wasn't because they were particularly fond of her. They only wanted to see her house. Ah BuKien had no problem with that arrangement – it was as well established a tradition as the rule that Asian youth never called their parents on the phone just to chat. Any departure from these tacit protocols would arouse deep suspicion.

Ah BuKien was more than happy to give us her sedulously self-critical tour. "See this," she said, pointing a finger at a breathtakingly beautiful Chinese wooden table. "My husband insisted that we buy it. I said to him, 'Oh, you stupid man with your tragic countryside tastes, this looks like a godforsaken coffin I wouldn't even put our ancestral relics' toenail clippings in!' But the peasant *insisted* that we buy it and do you know how much it cost? Do you? Have a guess. Guess."

And so the tour of the house continued, with Ah BuKien lamenting the cost of every item her husband had insisted thcy purchase, but first making us guess the price. My parents made sure their "guesses" were low enough, but not *too* low. After Ah BuKien hurled out the real price, we all courteously feigned cardiac arrest and my mother would exclaim, "Wah!"

"Wah indeed!" cried Ah BuKien.

Later, in the car driving home, my mother chattered endlessly about Ah BuKien's abysmal sense of style and how shamelessly she showed everything off. "And what about that carved coffin-table?" my father agreed. "Such peasant tastes."

"I thought it was quite beautiful," I said all of a sudden.

"You just watch it," my mother warned me, "you're beginning to acquire peculiar peasant tastes too." My parents abhorred anything that reminded them we would grow up yellow and there was nothing they could do to save us.

I had never met Ah BuKien's son. The day we visited her house, he was away being tutored. He had tutors for every subject. Ah BuKien showed off her boy in the same way she showed off her assets. "Woe, the school system here is not that good," she told my mother one day.

"But sister," my mother exclaimed, "I thought you sent your son to a private school."

"I did." But the boy didn't make it into medicine. She was incensed that she couldn't pay his way into the course. "Only a percentile of 92.4! The boy is a retard!"

Indeed, I wanted to add, *and this is the imbecile you expect me to marry?* I didn't even know his name. I only knew him as "Ah BuKien's son." Her rice-noodle boy – quivery, white and malleable, made exactly like her pasta. I was resolute in hating him. Even if he was Adonis Incarnate I would feel the same contempt for him.

All his sporting trophies were lined up behind glass in that heavy house of his. And his report card was mediocre for everything except physical education. It too was displayed behind the cabinet. I hated him even more – this was the type of boy who never gave me a second glance in high school, except when he needed work from me. I suspected that he hated me too. If, that is, he knew of his mother's intention. With all the pressure he was under, I wouldn't be surprised if her precious son was one of those boys who smoked pot behind the gymnasium in his blazer, going through life tormented by Oriental Oedipal agonies.

When we were about to leave her house, Ah BuKien said to my parents, "It is a pity you couldn't meet my son today." Then she squeezed my cheeks until I could feel the blood vessels erupting. The Cambodian Chinese liked their young girls to have cheeks as red as monkeys' bottoms. Already, she was endeavouring to mould me. Soon she even progressed to pinching me while I was at work.

At Footscray Retravision, there was a propensity for some mainland Chinese to refuse to buy items made in China. Whenever they said haughtily, *"O, zhongguo zuo de wo bu yao"* – I don't want anything made in China – I couldn't help myself. I would ask with salesgirl innocence, "But sir, aren't *you* made in China?" Of course, I always had to feign that little giggle that sounded like two brightly coloured balloons rubbing rapidly up against each other. Unlike my younger sisters, who grew up in tastefully bland pastel dresses, I had spent my childhood with a grandmother who packaged me into padded Mao suits and made me aware that I had to defend myself against all the other blandly dressed banana-children – children who were yellow on the outside but believed they could be completely white inside. My grandmother had warned me that those children grew up to become sour, crumple-faced lemons. I now believed her.

One day, I was explaining the functions of a Walkman to a customer when I felt someone twist the bare flesh of my upper arm. It hurt like hell. I turned around and there was that face – fierce eyes tattooed with permanent black liner, lashes sharpened with mascara. Each time she blinked, her eyes looked like two stygian insects in their death throes. "Agheare!" she said in a too-loud voice, "are you working here for the holidays?"

No, I'm just loitering about trying to pinch something for my dope addiction. I'm intending to sell some to your tormented boy too. My pimp will be here any moment now.

"Yes, Auntie," I replied, "can I help you with anything?" I wondered what product she was enquiring about. Whatever question she was going to ask, I would direct her to another sales assistant. My Walkman customer was getting impatient. I looked at Ah BuKien expectantly.

"What was your Year Twelve result?" she asked me.

I realised that the product she was after was *me*. She was assessing my desirability for her son – it was a sick kind of transferred lasciviousness. Returning to my customer, I simulated indifference to her scrutiny, but secretly I relished the thought that if she was searching for my child-bearing hips, she wouldn't find any.

Back at home, I told my parents about The Pinch. "She's just fond of you!" they laughed. Hell, if that was her way of showing affection, I wondered what she would do on my wedding night if she had her way. Probably hand her son a whip.

And if her plans were realised, she would make sure *everyone* attended the lavish banquet. I would be dressed in the same style as the Footscray wedding cake, crammed into a dress with too many frills, too much embroidery. No tasteful marzipan icing for Ah BuKien. No, I would be artificial cream fashioned into inedible roses. I would at least match their house. And of course, true to established custom, I would have to move into Ah BuKien's household. Ideal daughters-in-law were meant to suffer stoically, but I refused to be the moribund butterfly.

I suspected that my mother might have even been colluding with Ah BuKien, both of them plotting my descent into docility. When I was only a few months old, my mother had cut off my eyelashes, believing they would grow back thicker and longer. She must have done it while I was asleep with a pair of nail scissors. As a baby, there was already fault with me.

I felt that there were generations of stupid women conspiring against my liberty, and there seemed to be no escape. My mother was forever telling me to be careful. "Careful" translated literally in Chinese means to have a "small heart". I refused to have a small heart. "Be careful?" I wanted to retort. "Mother, you risked gouging out my eyeballs when I was a baby just so I could blink at boys! And now you're telling me that if I don't be careful I am going to turn into a slut?" The Cambodians have a saying: "A girl is like white cotton wool – once dirtied, it can never be clean again. A boy is like a gem – the more you polish it, the brighter it shines."

Their plan was already working. Whenever I was with a boy I could not stop the guilty look over the shoulder. It became a reflex. I was already turning into the timid ingénue devoid of all personality that Asian women considered the consummate ideal. My head-swivelling compulsion unsettled most boys. What could I tell them? "Nothing, Benjamin, just checking to see if my parents are charging up to attack you from behind with a cleaver" or "Don't worry, Phong, I usually convulse from the neck up when I am in love"?

I was expected to keep my eyes tightly shut until I was filed down to fine femininity. It seemed that anything I did of my own volition would shake up seven generations of dead ancestors and irrevocably damage the souls of the following seven. I couldn't care less about these stupid ancestors who were so resolute in crushing me. I dreamt of doing something that would make them turn in their graves and squish a decomposing eyeball.

Ah BuKien persisted with her insidious bartering. My parents ignored her completely. Every time we drove past that big white house in Footscray, I looked the other way. One day there came a second pinch at work.

"Oh Auntie," I said dully. "What would you like?" But my

mother also spotted Ah BuKien. They went to greet each other. I waited, pretending to dust electrical appliances so I could edge nearer to listen in on their conversation.

What does she have to say? I wondered. That her husband bought her son and me a king-sized coffin of a bed?

"Oh, how are you, sister?" my mother asked. "How is your husband? How is your house? How are your children? How are their studies going?"

Ah BuKien seemed to have lost her verbal facility for once. She didn't want to answer. Finally, she sighed. "My son doesn't go to school anymore." I was stunned. In the ensuing silence, I pretended I was dusting a toaster.

"So what is he doing now?" my mother asked.

"Working at the factory."

"What! You mean your rice-noodle factory?"

"Yes."

There was another silence. Then my mother responded quickly. "Oh, it's good that he is already able to help you earn money! My daughter is a great woe to us, she has five years of law to go!"

"Well," Ah BuKien finally said, "she may not be earning you money now, but wait until she graduates!"

"Ah BuKien and I were just talking," I heard my mother say to my father a little later. "Her boy is already helping her earn money at the factory."

"Oh, what a useful young man he is turning out to be!" smiled my father.

I was amazed at how skilled my parents were at acting out this pretence. I knew they believed that there was no redemption for Ah BuKien's son. Suddenly I felt very sorry for him.

His mother had truly moulded him into the consummate Rice-Noodle Boy. But I knew that her moulding days for me were now over, because before she left, she did not flatter me with a final pinch.

"**W**ow," he breathed as we emerged from the station onto the street. The sky was slowly turning the colour of a three-day-old bruise, and the streets were wet.

I stopped walking and turned to face him.

"Come on, please get back on the train and go home."

"Go home?" he cried in mock mortification, complete with hands-to-the-face demonstration. "Oh! I'm doing the chivalrous thing by escorting you back through these brutal streets and you tell me to nick off!"

"Well, I've managed for eighteen years by myself, I think I should be fine for one more day."

"Go home?" he cried. "You have no idea! I can't possibly go home."

"Yes, you can. You have a Daily Metcard which expires at 2 a.m."

"Ohhh, please don't make me go back! I can't!"

"Why not?"

"Because I have journeyed perilously by train to get here, wedged between disease-carrying passengers and surviving only by clinging to a hand-rail with three fingers! Please don't send me back! Oh, such suffering I have endured to get here!"

As moved as I was by his miserable odyssey, I had to tell him that *we* weren't parading our suffering by moaning about landmines and leaking boats.

"But that's because you're brave and strong. I'm just a poor orphan whose parents have not too recently died a slow and agonising death."

"Oh yeah? From what?"

"Complacency! Their bodies are decomposing in front of the television as we speak."

"Oh, how heartbreaking."

"Come on, if I told *you* to go home ..."

"If you told *me* to go home you'd be standing here naked and shoeless and sick. Remember, it's people like us who sew your jeans, make your runners and end up becoming your doctors. Besides, I *am* home."

"Want to hear a poem?"

"No."

"I made it up just for you."

"Err ... no thanks."

We walked past blurred aerosol graffiti written on the roller-shutters of the One Hour Photo Shop. The rain had painted the ground a dirty anthracite colour, and the sidewalk proudly displayed its shining black circles of ancient gum on the hard grey pages and pages of concrete.

The only other white boys around could hardly string a sentence together, let alone plead for temporary asylum. Empty-eyed, they loitered, wearing diarrhoea-coloured cargo pants and swearing loudly at every opportunity. Now they were staring at us.

I looked at my escort. It was bizarre how the scruffy college look that was so grungy at uni looked really derro here. In fact, he could fit right in if he tried to look drowsier and kept his mouth shut. When he opened his mouth, he killed off any chance of establishing lifelong friendships with the watchers across the road. And now they were beckoning us over – or, more accurately, beckoning *him* over.

"See what you've done?" I whispered. "Now they *really* think you're chasing, and they also probably think that I'm your girlfriend, so you're putting my life at risk every time I walk down these streets now."

I wasn't really scared, of course. In this suburb, I was more scared of interloping Indochinese "aunts" than the local drug-dealers, because the latter generally left me alone.

"Ummm … they want me to go over." He looked at me anxiously.

"Sure. Go over. They're going to invite you to their cock-tail party. Remember to pop into Forges to buy a tie before you cross the road."

"You're not much help," he muttered.

"I told you to go home, but you didn't take my advice. Board the train if you don't want to put your back-door virginity at risk."

"I'm not leaving you here alone! What do you think will happen?"

"Nothing. We've just been standing in the middle of the street talking for too long, and any two people who are station-ary for more than three minutes are suspected of carrying stuff. Remember, this is all your doing. Keep walking and ignore them."

As we kept walking, a stupid smirk appeared on his face.

"What's so funny?"

"Heh. Now that I've put your life at risk, I'm going to have to escort you back from the station to your father's shop every day."

My knight in shining aluminium foil, please don't feel it necessary to martyr yourself. My pa will kill you if he sees you. Thinking of my father, I walked a little slower.

"What time does your dad's shop close tonight?" he asked.

"Nine o'clock. It's Friday – late-night trading."

"Errr … it's only six-thirty at the moment." He had stopped in front of a shopfront with neon lettering on the outside declaring Hai Duong Vietnamese Noodles. Mr Hai Duong himself was probably inside declaring, "Wah, isn't that the Newtone Electronics daughter and what is she doing loitering with scruffy white demons?"

He looked at me. "Umm … want to grab some dinner then?"

I hesitated, and tried to think clearly.

He really likes you, I told myself.

No way, he likes the idea *of you*, the less feeble part of my mind insisted, *he's probably a sinophile. Don't forget that he's doing an Asian Studies major. You're like his third-world trip or something. He's too broke to go overseas so you're his substitute exotic experience. You go to dinner with him now and he'll think you're going to be his Cheery Chysanthemum forever, or at least until he gets bored of you and the next little Oriental Oleander comes along. Then you're going to be sorry.*

Bugger, what'll I do?

How the hell am I meant to know, I've never been on a "date"

222

before! But you're not going to last long if you keep using words like bugger, because authentic Chinese chicks don't speak like that, you sound like a bloody ocker.

Well, what am I supposed to do?

Firstly, stop having this dialogue inside your head because he'll realise that you're not only slow but insane too. Secondly, tell him no, tell him he's a show-off and a sinophile only interested in your ethnicity, tell him you don't do conventional Karate-Kid-Part-II *romances, tell him you have to head back before it gets dark, tell him you have to help your father sell Walkmans, tell him you have to go to the May Madness Sale at Forges to buy plastic tofu boxes for your mother, tell him you have to go to the local pool before closing time to check out those fabulous homeboys getting changed into their flannelette shirts and trousers before they retreat back to their com-pu-tahs, tell him you have to find a way to dispose of those prying Indochinese interlopers who will stare at you and report back to your relatives when you eventually tell him …*

"Umm, yeah, okay."

Bugger.

After all, what's the big deal? I reasoned to myself, *have some humility. A young man casually mentions that you might have dinner together and you think he's asking for your hand, you think you're going to end up being his little Indochinese wife and in a decade's time you won't be fascinating enough any more because he's just drawn to the idiosyncrasies of your culture, and he has no idea that your culture extends to looking after your folks in their decrepit dotage and constantly looking out for ASIO which has caused you to develop a nasty compulsive head-swivelling habit. And of course he has no idea that ASIO really stands for Asian (Southeast) Investigation Organisation, but if you tell him, perhaps one day when you've both graduated, he can help you sue the organisation for causing you chronic pain and suffering ...*

I was still not convinced.

Oh, come on, Voice of Reason cajoled, *you're turning into one of those anxious killjoy Asian women who worry so much that they end up with dried-fig faces at the age of thirty; come on, you're only eighteen, just sit down, just relax, just have dinner, and don't take things so seriously.*

So we entered the mirror-walled, plastic Ikea-chaired surroundings of Hai Duong, and when we sat down, he asked me: "What will your father say when I ask you to be my girlfriend?"

*

My cousin Melanie had recently married her skip boyfriend, although I don't know why he called himself that. "Hey I'm just a skip!" he kept insisting, "I won't be offended if you all call me that, ha ha!" He grinned like a goof at his own generosity, not realising that all my other relatives had already determined from day one that they would refer to him as the Round Redhaired Demon, even in Melanie's presence. They congratulated themselves on their own magnanimity of spirit – after all, we were well known for calling "our own people" such affectionate names as "Horseface", "Toothless Aunt", "Duck Brother" and "Big Fat Potato".

Big Fat Potato was the boy to whom I was to have been betrothed according to the whims of his mother. When that hadn't worked out, she quickly put him on a plane to Vietnam and he came back with better goods. Oh, much better! The girl was beautiful and shy and sweet, and I wondered whether she knew she had ended up with the son of a Permanent Pincher. Perhaps she didn't know. Perhaps he seduced her with a suitcase loaded with Ferrero Rocher chocolates and Gloweave shirts.

I was not invited to the wedding, of course, so the first time I ever met Big Fat Potato was when I accompanied my mother to the Grand Opening of his mother's new grocery store. There I saw a skinny young man with his chin almost touching his chest, watching the register. He looked like a sad squid with a big head. "Ay." His mother grabbed him by the shoulders and glared at me: "This is Tim." Her chin was as high as her son's was low, and she thrust him forward as if to say, *Look here, this is what you could have had if your parents didn't think you were too good for him. Now that he's married, your snobby old man has not only lost a son-in-law but also a Chinese Grocery Store, mwwaahhh hah hah, go suck lychees and dieeee!*

I barely glanced at the son, as if to say, *Dear Aunt, you can shove durians up your Chinese Grocery Store for all I care.*

"Hello," I muttered.

He glared at me with lowered eyes, as if to say, You *are the one my ma thought would make me a good wife, so you must be a traditional tea-pouring, tale-telling bitch and I hate you.*

"Hi," he mumbled.

Should I ask questions? I wondered. "How is your wife?" No, too personal. *How did* you *know about my wife, you gloating gossip?* "How's business? Must be good working here hah?" *I'm stuck at my mother's store selling Vietnamese beef jerky, how do* you *think business is?* "Having fun at the counter?" *Ecstatic fun, would you like me to dance the merry little "Buy Korean Gingseng" jig for you?*

Fortunately, my mother broke the silence by exclaiming, "Wah! Your son! Married now! And your daughter-in-law is so beautiful, so useful, so helpful, so good!" Too bad the girl couldn't hear these compliments because she was packing boxes in the back room.

"You know," my mother said, "my niece got married recently too, but she married a white ghost. I always tell my daughter never to pick one of them because you know how they tend to sleep around."

"Oh, but they're not *all* like that. Also, having a white son-in-law could be good," declared Fat Potato's mother, "more people kowtow to you, you know."

Of course. Melanie's father knew that very well. We could never escape the counter-effects of colonisation, they were passed on two generations and more. "When Melanie takes the Round Red-Headed Demon back to Cambodia for the honeymoon, they will be swamped by kowtowers from all sides, heh heh!" boasted Uncle Frank. He loved his new son-in-law as much as his own child. The white skin did the trick. The white skin would ensure that Uncle Frank got the respect his own small sense of self denied him. We were funny that way, always believing that we were rescued by white people even when the white people didn't see themselves as our rescuers – in fact, they probably thought that we were self-sufficient, hard-working heroes from Hanoi or Hunan who manufactured their T-shirts and married their sons.

But we were also hypocrites. We loved them for their easy-going natures, their laid-back generosity, their simple acceptance of our culture, or whatever we told them constituted our culture. We fed them fluorescent yellow lemon chicken and sludge-black beef in black-bean sauce and they lauded our fine Chinese cuisine. Anything nuanced, like brown braised chicken's feet (we were never wasteful) was also cultural but in an idiosyncratic "only the Chinese eat that" sort of way. We loved their country, their supermarkets and their sheer genius in inventing Glad-Wrap; and the more we loved these things, the more it made us realise how much we hated the dirt, the sludge and the smells of our homelands, the squelchy grottiness of our markets and the self-abnegation of our souls.

But most of all, we hated ourselves for loving them.

*

I grabbed a paper napkin from the metal napkin box on the table and started wiping my spoon and chopsticks with it. Then I started wiping his utensils.

His eyes widened. "Umm, what do you think you're doing?"

"Saving you from Mr Salmonella."

"Isn't that a bit rude?"

"Look around you. Everone else is doing it. That's what these napkins are for. The restaurant owners don't care. Saves their poor high-school sons from having to wash the dishes too thoroughly. We're actually doing them a favour."

He didn't look too convinced, but he saw that at least three other tables were doing the same. He also noticed for the first time the fourteen-year-old son of the owner, still sweating in his white shirt with his private-school tie loosened around his neck, taking orders from the table opposite us. He turned back to me. "So ... umm, how about it?" His eyes, I noticed, were the same colour as the amber jar of fish-sauce on the table.

I liked fish-sauce.

I didn't know what to say or do, and it was my turn to speak. What could I say? *"How about* what*?"* *Come on, you know exactly what what implies, you're just prolonging his torment.* *"Oh. You want to go out with me. Sure. Get in line, and get your folks to make an inventory of their assets and real estate, including any small businesses they own, and then get them to put forward a tender submission to my folks."* *Or how about,* *"I'd love to be your girlfriend, but my darling, first you need to get a bowl haircut, you need to get a shirt-and-tie combo, you need to stop making up silly sonnets and start thinking about our mortgage and how you can give my parents Eurasian grandkids so that we can improve the gene pool for the next generation, because Eurasians are meant to be the most beautiful people in the world according to my pa,* The Reader's Digest *and* Han Suyin*."*

Then I thought about Cousin Melanie parading her husband around to our dirt-poor relatives in Phnom Penh and it wasn't so funny anymore. I suddenly felt very sad, and not so good about myself.

He just wants to screw you and sow his wild oats, I told myself, *and then not even the Fresh-off-the-Boats at Footscray Swim Centre will want you, and all your eggs will dry up and you'll be a sorry case, a warning to future delinquent daughters. And then what will you do hah?*

I didn't know what to do. I remembered once unpacking a new washing machine for a middle-aged customer. He stood admiring the product, nodding his approval. "I could get one for half the price at Cash Converters, but there's nothing like brand-new goods, you mark my words, young lady. Cost me a week's wages, but worth it. Brand-new." And then: "That's how we Chinese like our women too." Wink wink, nudge nudge. I imagined the neat young homeboys with their severe expressions and their shirts tucked into their pants diligently packing me into a cardboard box, sealing the top with masking tape and sending me back to my manufacturers. "No good, is broken." And their mothers standing over them, boxing their ears and shouting, "Aiyah, stupid boy! How could you pick one that was broken hah?" Hands shoved in their pockets and looking sheepish, they would protest, "But Ma, how was I to know? She *did* sell us a new microwave, remember?"

I started to laugh. *Good, good, treat it as a joke, because you're taking this whole thing far too seriously. Laugh so that you won't squirm when he says, "I was only kidding, hah hah, I just came back with you to meet Franco Cozzo," or when he tells you, "Heh, what a joke, I was only mucking around, hasn't your mother ever told you that we white devils do that all the time, we get our kicks that way?", or when he says …*

"I *am* serious, you know."

Oh.

How serious? I immediately wanted to ask. I told myself to shut up.

Come on, Voice of Reason coaxed, *just say yes. Come on, look at him, he's cute, and other girls like him, and he doesn't seem the type of boy who's going to make you wear Hello-Kitty apparel or hold his hand because helplessness is so endearing, and oh, come on, he has fish-sauce eyes for crying out loud!*

But I couldn't stop the other commentary that was going on inside my mind. I wanted to ask him whether he planned to go to Southeast Asia anytime soon, because there he would meet girls ten thousand times nicer and milder and good-er than I was, girls like Big Fat Potato's wife who would graciously slink into the corners and sit in back rooms grateful just to be here. Girls who would dote on him, who'd do more than wipe the salmonella from his spoon and fork.

I wanted to know whether he wanted to go out with me just to spite his parents. To say, look here, you Capital-L Liberal folks, I'm different from you, I'm going out with this authentic, culturally oppressed ethnic minority, and she's going to give our kids the third-world gene, and there is nothing you can do about it! Then I realised that if I still had head lice and scabies he would not have given me a second glance.

I wanted to know whether it was only because I was "exotic", and if so, what that word meant to him. If he told me he liked my almond eyes and caramel skin, I would tell him to buy a bag of confectionery instead, because I was sick of it all – how we always had to have hair like a black waterfall, alabaster or porcelain skin, and some body part or other resembling a peach. I wanted to ask him whether one of his reasons for going out with me was to test out the rumour about Asian girls' gynaecological advantages. And finally, I wanted to know why, out of all the girls in his college who liked him, he had picked me.

But then I thought, bugger it. I didn't want to marry him. And if I didn't want to marry him, then why go through all the trouble and torment for something so impermanent? Dating – my Auntie Chia's first and only "date" was at thirty-two, in *Safeway*, and she had been sent there by my grandparents to suss out whether her fiancé was a cheapskate. Why should I even *give it a try*? Soon enough he would discover that I wasn't the flippant, fun or exciting girl he liked, especially with the head-swivelling compulsion and the multiple neuroses. Going out with him would transform me into Woody Allen with a black wig. In half a decade's time I would be someone's serious wife, and he would be history because we Southeast Asians don't do the *Bridges of Madison County* thing. Or perhaps in half a decade's time I would have the matchmakers avoiding me like the plague, whispering to each other, "Oh, there's the one who does the dating thing, goes out with one after another to try them out."

I didn't know which was worse. I could already feel the ASIO spies disguised as diners watching me.

Bugger it, why couldn't I have something simple and spontaneous and not-so-serious? Bugger. Bugger. Bugger. Then I realised, why not? Just give him a simple and spontaneous and not-so-serious answer to show him that you're a simple and spontaneous and not-so-serious person. Why not why not why not?

"No."

"What do you mean, no?"

"I can't." *Great. Now you sound like fifteen-year-old loser whose parents won't let her go out. What are you going to say now? "It's not you, it's* me*?" Oh, but it was so true!*

We both sat there looking pretty tormented. When our food arrived, we let the noodles soak. He half-heartedly plonked in a spoon.

"You know, I don't know how to do this."

"Don't worry, they automatically lower the MSG content for Caucasians and you can use a fork."

"No! I mean, I've never … you know, asked anyone … like … well, you know …"

"Oh."

"Perhaps I've gone about it the wrong way. I'm an idiot. Sorry. I've mucked it up. Crap."

"No, you haven't. I think *I've* mucked it up." I paused, and realised that I didn't say these words merely to make him feel better either. I wanted to cry. This was terrible and confusing and I had mucked it up by thinking too much, and now I had hurt this poor amateur Asian-asker-outer by frightening myself with fears before anything had even happened.

"Well …" I said, and paused. Where could I begin?

"Err …" I began again. How could I begin? Oh, what to say! Oh, what to do!

Luckily he came up with a simple solution.

"Ummm … can we un-muck it then?"

Anything to get rid of this sudden sinking feeling I had in my gut, this feeling of cowardice. This feeling of missing out on something I wasn't even sure I wanted. But worst of all, this feeling of missing out on something I might have chosen for myself.

"Okay."

ONCE we resolved to un-muck things, it became much easier. After all, I thought, it was time to loosen this small and tightly coiled life of mine and do the things that ordinary young people did, like falling in love without being under the spotlight of the Indochinese (in)security cameras. So I went on my first date. And my second and third. Woohoo, I thought, I'm doing well. At least I beat Aunt Chia's record, and in none of those dates did we venture near a supermarket. In fact, I didn't even let my parents know I was "going out", and we visited places and suburbs where no one would ever recognise us.

"Got to go to Mao-Bin U library today," I declared to my mother on the days I was not supposed to be at university. There were no questions asked, because I was trading on my reputation as a studious daughter. University was a foreign country to my parents. Never having set foot inside one, they saw universities as little scaled-down cities populated with the best and finest minds. "My daughter is studying at Mao-Bin U," my mother declared to her friends, especially ones who also had sons studying there. Their pronunciation made the place sound like a shonky university in China for discarded communists, but our proud Southeast Asian mothers spoke the name with such reverence that it hardly mattered.

"Don't come home too late." By too late my mother meant anytime past 6 p.m.

"I won't."

*

"Have you ever hopped on a random train and got off at a place you have never been before?" I asked him.

"No."

I often looked at the signs on stations while travelling past on trains and tried to imagine what those places might be like. I pictured Balaclava as a place full of thugs and Box Hill as full of packing crates. Sometimes I hopped off at arbitrary places and had a wander around, pretending I was an overseas student by speaking slowly to strangers. I always wanted to get off at another destination, to escape the familiarity of home and be anonymous, an adventurer. So there we were on our first date, sitting on the bright green grass in the middle of an empty equestrian park in Caulfield.

We were both unfamiliar with the suburbs of Melbourne, because he had come from the countryside and I had spent most of my life locked in two neighbourhoods. "Your neighbourhood is fascinating," he told me, lying on the grass, hands behind his head, staring up at the sky. "Even without English, the people there seem to understand each other so well that they could get to work on the Tower of Babel again with no problems."

I sat cross-legged, back straight. I realised that no matter how tired or how hot, I could never be so laid-back, even if no one else was around. Would I ever see the sky as completely and as clearly as he could? I was always on guard, always ready

234

to leap to my feet and deny everything. *Boy? What boy? I'm not with any boy! I'm a good girl, saving myself up for some whitegoods connoisseur who will treat me like a brand-spanking-new fridge.* Then I heard my mother's voice in my head – *those Aussie boys, they just park themselves anywhere, and sprawl their limbs in every direction, you had better watch out.*

But I was acting less and less like a top-notch Frigidaire model the more we spoke. I became less fidgety. I stopped pulling blades of grass from the ground and realised that I had cleared quite a large patch. *A few more outdoor dates,* I thought, *and Jim's Mowing would be out of business.*

"Speaking of bible stories," I said, "I was brought up to believe that the fall of man was Adam's fault entirely."

"Really? Even though I've never met your mother, somehow I don't imagine her as a raving feminist."

"Not my mother. My father. He used to tell me stories when I was small. His version of the Fall-from-Paradise story went something like this: Adam stands in the garden of Eden and reaches out for the apple on the tree. 'Don't pick it!' Eve cries out to him, but Adam takes a big bite out of the apple, offering it to Eve, who, of course, refuses. Suddenly a huge voice roars from the sky, 'Hey, what the *HELL* do you think you're doing, Adam?' Adam is so startled that he chokes on his piece of apple and it gets stuck in his throat. The Lord then decides that that's pretty funny, and it should be stuck there permanently as evidence of Adam's guilt. So that's my father's explanation of why men have Adam's apples." I looked down at him, because here in this unknown area I could look him straight in the face without having to avert my eyes or be demure. "Hey, that's strange, because you don't appear to have an Adam's apple."

"Yes, I do."

"Nah, I don't think so. I think without the obvious mark of Deity disobedience you are destined to be a celibate of sorts. Which means you shouldn't even be here with me."

"No, it's here. Feel here."

Suddenly he had taken my hand and placed it at his throat and my fingers were so stunned that they became still and stuck. *Move, hand!* I commanded, *move move move stupid fingers!*

No.

What do you mean no?!

Actually, we like it here.

What are you saying?

We're going on strike, piped up the pinkie.

Yeah that's right, said the pointer, *a digital revolution, you could call it.*

Because my fingers were so immobile, all the little nerve endings shot to the surface, sensitive that this was someone else's skin. My mind went completely blank. All the feeling I had became concentrated in this one hand, these four entranced digits and this non-opposing thumb.

Searching for remnants of primeval fruit lodged in the throat of a loved one was not the most conventionally romantic or titillating experience an eighteen-year-old girl could dream up, but this was the first time I had made physical contact with a member of the opposite sex who was past the potty-training stage. Growing up, I was never the type of girl to give a boy a little playful push on the shoulder or a shove towards the sprinklers. But here I was, with my hands at his throat, and I could feel his pulse beneath my fingertips. This is wonderful! I thought. Boys weren't scary at all, I realised, there really was nothing to fear – in fact, if I pressed a bit harder I was sure that I could make his eyeballs pop out of his head! But I was afraid that I might hurt him, or that my hands were too cold; and hoping that the ecstatic surprise was not too evident on my face.

"What a very nice neck you have," I blurted out. *What an idiot you are*, I said to myself, *he's going to think you're some sort of neck-ophiliac now. And besides, boys are meant to make comments about women's throats, not the other way around. Quick, quick, balance it out with some comment about his nice eyes, his nice smile, his nice earlobes! Help, what do I say next?* I wondered, *Help! I don't know the rules!*

Then I thought, *Bugger the rules. I always get them wrong anyway.*

So I removed my fingers from his neck with feigned indifference and told him about growing up in Braybrook and working under the supervision of madcap relatives with laser-beam eyes. I couldn't seem to stop talking. Almost everything I said sounded fascinating to friends at university, but sometimes I felt as if I was some sort of permanent exchange student, as if they were only interested in me for what little idiosyncrasy I could offer them. This time I decided not to offer any idiosyncrasies. I decided to tell it as it was.

"Your life sounds amazing," he said.

"Not as amazing as yours – travelling around all of Australia, and being able to go anywhere in the world that takes your fancy. You've really … *lived*."

"No, *you've* really lived."

We had both lived very different lives. How did we end up here, together, in this park in the middle of nowhere? I felt life open up for me – all the different directions I could go. The suffocating prospect of being stuck in a tiny two-person legal practice up above a shop in suburbia ten years from now shattered, and all the pieces fell down like fake snow from a smashed glass paperweight. The water splashed on my face, it seemed to wake me from the deep sleeping sickness. I felt exhilarated. I could be anywhere, and I could do anything. I could be anybody I wanted. My small windowed world exploded in colour and light and little pieces of broken glass. *So what if I get a few cuts*, I thought, *a few cuts are nothing compared to feeling like a dead weight.*

"Did you always want to be a law student?" he asked me.

"No," I admitted, "when I was very young I wanted to be an artist. Later I wanted to be a teacher. I never thought that it was possible for me to get into law. But now that I am in, I think it is the best thing that could have happened to me. People come to me with letters they can't read, contracts they can't understand, and they put their complete trust in an eighteen-year-old. I feel so … useful. Because they've never been there themselves, the older generation think that everything we learn at university is sacred and practical." I laughed. "They have no idea we spend six months doing Derrida. And to tell the truth, I don't even *understand* Derrida! One day I'm going to wake up and realise that this French fogey held all the answers to solving the legal tenure of my cousin's bakery in St Albans, and then I will regret being such a philistine."

He laughed.

I turned to him. "What about you? Why did you study law?"

"Do you want the honest truth?"

238

"Yes."

"Back in Year Ten, I watched *Gandhi*."

We stayed in companionable silence for a long time, until he sat back up and looked at the sky. "It's going to get dark soon. You'd better leave before your tracking device goes off." I had always to leave my mobile phone on so that my father could call me at any time. "Don't you feel frustrated sometimes? You're eighteen and you have to be home before the sun sets. That's six o'clock in winter and eight o'clock in summer!"

I didn't know how to respond to that. Of course I felt frustrated at times. Of course I felt the unfairness of it all. I knew better than my parents, who saw me as prey for predatory men. *Lock up your daughters or lose them!* seemed to be their motto. *You must encourage your daughter to become a top-notch barrister, a community leader, the future Lord Mayor of Melbourne even. You must teach her that in her abilities, she is just as talented and able as the young men in this country. But whatever you do, you must make sure she is not exposed to any of them. Better yet, you must make sure that she doesn't have to make any choices about men in her life. She can't handle it, she'll just make big mistakes.*

But I also knew that no one was going to have any confidence in a future leader who walked around in small circles being scared of the dark. The potential barrister would only ever end up a meek clerk who clocked off at 5.30. The potential mayor would end up a secretary, and the potential independent young woman would end up being seen by outsiders as a sad case of cultural oppression. That was not who I was at all! How dare he feel sorry for me!

"I'm not afraid of the dark, you know."

"Of course you're not. But we'd better get you home in time before your father blows it."

I glared at him with a blazing intensity which I did not know I was even capable of, and spoke slowly and quietly, trying to control myself. "Listen, I don't mind if you ask me to think about how irritating it is to be treated like an eleven-year-old princess and being locked up after 6 p.m. I don't even mind if you suggest that I follow or defy the rules. But don't – ever – give me that patronising 'poor you' look!"

"But … I wasn't."

I looked at him long and hard. Then I realised that he was telling the truth.

"I just want to get you home in time so your parents don't put you under house arrest and I can't see you again."

"Oh." Now I really felt like an eleven-year-old princess who had thrown an embarrassing tantrum. Why was I acting this way? I felt such anger, but I couldn't direct it towards anyone. Both this boy and my father were so well intentioned. But something was still wrong. I couldn't figure out what it could be. Perhaps it was me.

"You make me feel so happy," he told me as he took me to the station.

It must be me, I determined.

"**W**HEN do you think I should meet your parents?"

It was time for me to sober up. I knew it was too good to last, these four weeks of rapture.

"Soon," I replied.

"Have you told them?"

"No."

"Have you lied to them?"

"Lie to my parents? Could I bring myself to do such a thing?"

"You're lying by omission," he said matter-of-factly.

"Well, my parents haven't asked me anything yet, so I'm not lying."

He looked at me, expectant.

"I will tell my parents. This week in fact," I decided. "Are you scared?" I asked him.

"Petrified."

"Don't be smart."

"I'm not."

I looked at him and saw he was serious. His eyebrows were knotted, and he went all quiet. I recognised that composure from somewhere before, it seemed so familiar. Then I realised that I had seen it in myself. At that moment I realised how much I adored him.

I tried to be reassuring. "It'll be okay."

"It'll be just *okay*?" He looked disappointed. "Not 'Immortal Beloved, they will love you and offer you a house, a large dowry and a place at the head of the table'?"

"Immortal Beloved, they will love you and offer to castrate you if you ever do anything untoward, and what's more, the young man's side of the family are meant to be the ones who give the dowry."

"Can't believe this. I'm scared of your parents and I haven't met them yet! And they're probably going to be a metre shorter than me and half my weight."

I thought, if I were a young man I would be scared of my parents too. Perhaps not my father so much, because he was able to sit down and reason things out. But my mother – there was no way she would be able to understand an alien, let alone an alien her own daughter had chosen. My mother saw the differences as insurmountable – she was only comfortable with the familiar, yet she still believed that Princess Diana was the most dazzling creature ever to grace the earth, and that white women were more beautiful than we could ever be.

She would often watch television and point in astonishment at any display of affection between parents and their grown children. "Wah," she would exclaim, "even though the parents chuck their kids out of home after they leave school, and even though the kids chuck the parents in nursing homes after they leave work, they still seem to display some sort of love toward each other. Amazing." Or she would see an ad for soft drinks and cry, "Incredible, those white ghosts! Look, that one has her bellybutton showing and she's even got an earring in there!

How depraved can you get?!" Or watching a Werther's toffee ad: "That little boy gave his grandpa a toffee! And look, now the grandpa is smiling with a full set of white teeth and taking the toffee! Oh, now the grandpa is eating the toffee and they both look really happy." Her comments were like those of a scientist observing slides under the microscope: "Wah, these little amoeba are fascinating, some of them have a nucleus of gold."

*

There was a simplicity about my mother's face, a stillness about her stretched-straight mouth and eyes. If you were to film it, nothing much would happen. You'd have to place the camera on a tripod, sit and wait. Bang around a few pots, make sound effects. Perhaps your camera would catch a few blinks, a blank look, a bewildered "ay, turn that thing off" and a jab of finger zooming towards the lens, but nothing more. You watch the home videos your father made, and as sure as day it always happens. "Ay, what do you think you are doing? Turn it off!" she says.

But there is only so much the camera can catch. It does not capture the times when she laughs, her head flung back, nostrils flared, like a happy hippopotamus with squinched-closed eyes and blunt teeth, a few of them missing. When her teeth were falling out, she warned me not to invite any friends over until she had false ones fitted. She had one of those faces that hid nothing. When she was angry, her face would literally darken. It was terrifying. Just one expression, one look could make you feel like there was nothing between your backbone and the skin of your stomach.

Firstly, you knew that she was angry by her look, features set as if carved in anthracite stone. "So, you think you can just take a day off from work whenever you feel like it?" There was no use protesting that you had worked every day for the past two weeks. No one needed a day off, and there was no way that you could be tired, because she never was. She might get exhausted, but never weary. "Rest? Who needs rest? Tiredness doesn't matter." She pushed herself to the limit and had been doing so for two decades now; she knew no other way to live. And there was no use telling her that you wanted to spend a day alone with your boyfriend. "Alone? Why do you need time alone with him? What are you going to get up to?"

Secondly came the suspicion. "What do you do alone anyway?"

"Nothing."

"Then you don't need to spend any time alone!"

You knew she was only lonely, and frightened, scared of a potential son-in-law who spoke a language she couldn't understand. The two of you could be conspirators, in fact, the whole entire family could be – everyone seemed to understand one another except her. Perhaps she thought that she was not clever enough, not fast enough in her mind for this new world.

But in her work, she was the fastest person I knew. Always doing three things at once, she would have dinner ready in fifteen minutes flat – three dishes and a soup, and the dishes never repeated themselves the following day.

"Does he like our food?" she asked, meaning, did he at least eat the fluorescent lemon chicken in the touristy part of China-town? The trouble started on their first meeting, when I told her that he was a vegetarian. It was her birthday, and I had asked him to come to meet the entire family for the first time at the Dragon Boat Restaurant.

"No meat at all?" she asked. "Buddhist? Taoist? Why doesn't he eat meat?"

I paused. "Because he feels sorry for the animals." I was repeating his exact words, but echoed to my mother, they no longer sounded endearingly compassionate. They sounded stupid.

"Never heard such nonsense in my life. Back in Cambodia people are scrambling for food scraps on the floor!" I knew what she was thinking. *How spoilt. How like one of those people who live inside their head.* "Put some proper food on his plate," she ordered me. "He's skin and bones!"

I dutifully shovelled vegetables on top of his rice.

"I can eat prawns too," he told me as a concession.

I plopped some prawns on top.

"And chicken."

"Oh, I didn't know that."

"Well, I do. Bring it on."

I heaped the chicken slivers onto his plate.

"And crocodile."

On went the croc.

"And venison, too."

"Poor Bambi, eh?" I looked at him.

"Oh, I love Bambi," he raved. "He tastes just like chicken."

"That *was* chicken. I haven't given you any deer yet."

"Oh."

"Would you like some?"

"Yes please." I had never seen a more eager carnivore.

"Michael, I am impressed by the way you handle chopsticks," said my father. Why did they expect every non-Asian to be a bumbling jab-you-in-the-eye fool with chopsticks, and why was a twenty-year-old Caucasian's use of chopsticks something to clap about when little Chinese three-year-olds were using them like finger extensions? Why were white people so proud of their chopstick-wielding skills instead of seeing the abysmally low standards we had set for them?

"Wah, where did you learn that?" asked my father. "Just like an expert!"

"Thank you, Mr Pung," he said modestly.

There was, of course, no "Oh, just call me Bob/Joe/Jack, mate" from my father. My father's idea of getting familiar with someone was to tell them war stories. He didn't do it to sober them up or edify them, he did it to crack them up.

"This fish reminds me of the Pol Pot years when the starved, dead bodies floated up the river during the flood. I got the job of dragging them to higher, drier land. We wrapped them up in a dry blanket and me and my mate grabbed on to each end. Every time we tripped, the blanket would get water-soaked and even heavier. Hah hah, so funny! There we were, both probably only weighing seventy kilos between us, trying to drag this dead body three times our weight, and listen to this – my mate turns to me and says, 'Hope you're not going to be this heavy when it's time for me to drag you,' and I say to him, 'What do you mean when *you* drag *me*? I'm going to be the poor soul who will be dragging you!'"

Unfortunately, most of his guests had no idea whether to laugh or cry.

"Eat more fish!" my father would urge, "eat more fish!",

246

heaping it onto their plates. He did not believe in mental images leaving a bitter aftertaste. At home, whenever I told him not to mention certain things at the dinner table, he said, "I'm just talking about crap, you're not actually eating it!" But here was this boy, eating at least six species of native and domestic fauna just to please my parents. What a champ you are, I thought, those animals did not die in vain after all.

When it was time to present the gifts we had bought for my mother, my brother gave her a handbag. My sisters gave her things they had made – a little gold-sprayed macaroni frame and thingo to hang on the door. The thingo had Alison and Alina's photograph glued to it. I gave her a new shirt. And Michael pulled out a bunch of flowers – little white jasmines wrapped in tasteful brown paper and tied with a raffia ribbon. "Tanks you velly march," said my ma politely. I should have reminded him that the more garish the paper, the better, especially if it was bright red. My mother didn't understand that sometimes the more understated things cost the most. All she knew was that the bigger and brighter, the better. Of course, she would rather have had a durian.

"I didn't know what was appropriate," he said to her. "I even asked the gardener at college, and he told me to get these."

My mother didn't answer because she didn't understand a word he said. So I answered for her. "Oh, they are lovely. She loves them."

Does she like me? I knew he was thinking, *I don't know what she is thinking and she never gives me an answer when I speak to her. But on the other hand, she seems to be smiling a bit so that must be a good sign. I hope.*

I gave his hand a little squeeze under the table to reassure him of the lie he had been duped into believing.

*

I was well aware of my mother's list of objections to potential husbands. Don't marry an Aussie, they sleep around and have no morals. Don't marry a Cantonese, they will gamble away the family fortune. Don't marry a Vietnamese because they are charmers and spend too much. Don't marry a Teochew because they are stingy and spend too little. But whatever you do, you must not remain unmarried! So now she was going to elaborate on her objections against my going out with a white boy, clause by clause, a week after their first meeting. "I bet he splits everything in half," she began, "they are no good the way they do that. It means they can leave whenever they want. Does he split things in half?"

"No," I lied. The truth was, I also hated splitting bills in half. You either kept to yourself or gave it your all. One way was a way to conduct your affairs so that you minimised loss. The other way was built on hope and love and longevity, things that the accountants and actuaries could not calculate.

"Some non-Asians," I said, very careful with my words, "like to split things in half because they think that it is true equality."

"Hah! Equality! What kind of relationship is determined by a calculator? Does he calculate things like that?"

"No." This time I was speaking truthfully, because I made sure there was never an opportunity to calculate. I didn't want any arguments about money. Whenever we had to pay for something, I'd make sure my wallet was out.

"You know, your Auntie Que had a suitor once who always walked a few metres away when they were at the checkout of a supermarket. Your grandmother gave him the evil eye, but he was so thick he never got it. Then she started making comments about how expensive bok choy was these days."

Yes, I thought, these little tests to prove whether you could live with the person for the rest of your life. I was not ready for that yet, I did not even look for these things.

"Another thing, they are not as hard-working as we are," my mother continued. "You don't want to end up supporting your husband."

I wondered what was worse, being supported by your husband or supporting him. I thought of those women at home stuck between their four walls and their husband's whims, calling their spouse "Elder Brother" and fighting a daily war against dirt so that their pretend brother could come home to a clean house.

"Those Aussies, they see marriage as a light affair. You piss them off, they divorce you. And they hug and kiss other women all the time, like it means nothing."

I had met some of his female friends – girls with names like Cathy and Gemma and Louisa – girls who gave him big bear-hugs and kisses when they met. It was an Aussie thing, I decided. It was all innocent standard practice and it didn't mean a thing. *They* didn't have *issues* with physical contact like we did. Also, I didn't want those amicable, easygoing girls to think that I was Michael's Keeper – one of those little Asian chicks dressed all in black, glaring out of immaculately mascara-ed eyes and getting out the claws whenever another female came within three kilometres of her property. Cathy was an Arts/Science student with an earring through her eyebrow and Gemma wore long dyed Indian sari-skirts and wanted to be a third-world feminist.

If they had any respect for you, they would ease up on the kissing part, you know, I told myself, *after all, you're his girlfriend.*

No, you idiot, it's not them, I reprimanded myself, *it's you! You're just too uptight.*

But at least I don't go around kissing other people's boyfriends in full view of their girls! Perhaps some of what my mother said is true.

Don't be stupid, you know she's just working from broken stereotypes. You want to take the advice of someone who gleans their wisdom from Werther's toffee ads? Believe me, if you were his Australian girlfriend, you wouldn't have an issue at all with this.

How do you know? So you think maybe it is a cultural thing, their touchy-feely tendencies? Perhaps I should ask him about it …

NO!

Why not?

Because then he will know that you are insecure! That you blow little things into big grotesque carnival floats that cast shadows over perfect summer afternoons.

Well, who do I turn to? Who can tell me whether the kissing is something they do all the time to mates or whether they're just doing it because I'm his quiet little Asian chick who doesn't like to cause a ruckus? If Gemma's so interested in third-world women's rights then she should understand and respect us, damn her to her hemp hell! What can I do?

Accept it, the supposedly rational side of my mind advised me, *if you can't beat them or join them, then be "yourself". Asian women are meant to be legendary in their patience and calm in such matters, aren't they? Sit back stoically with an indulgent glint in your eye and he will love you ten times more for your generosity.*

Hang on there! I objected. *Something is not quite right …*

Shut up, you're meant to be practising your Zen tranquillity so that he will love you even more.

"Are you listening to me?" demanded my mother. "Honestly, I don't know what's going to become of you. You sit there like a bloody taro when I am trying to teach you important things, and it's as if you can't hear a thing! Must be diseased with love – your brain has turned to rot!"

"Ma, they're not all like that, you know," I told her.

"Like *that*, like *that*," she sighed, "you know, you're beginning to be like *that* too."

*

I didn't know what being like *that* was, but it was making my life progressively worse. Whenever we walked past her friends in Footscray, the jewellery-store wives behind their glass counters, they would ask the inevitable question – "Wah, daughter so big now! Does she have a boyfriend yet?"– and my mother would tell them "No."

I wanted to interject, but instead I smiled through gritted teeth until I could feel my face ossifying. She was only doing her duty as my mother to package and sell me as best as she could. She would not acknowledge that this package might have already been bought.

After many stormy looks in my direction, she exploded at the dinner table one evening. "Ah Hua saw your daughter kissing Michael!" she proclaimed to my father. She did not speak to me, but gesticulated wildly, doing a pretty good impersonation of her friend Ah Hua, except seventy decibels louder than the original: "'Wah', Ah Hua said to me, 'Sister, didn't you say they were just friends? They seem very close for friends.'"

Goddamn idle scuttlebutts! I thought. Bloody rumour-starter. She'll be sorry.

"When was this?" I demanded.

"At your sister's seventh birthday."

"You mean at Alina's birthday last weekend? *In this house?*" I was flabbergasted. Woah, this Ah Hua was getting delusional as well. What a sick mind.

"How am I meant to know where?"

I tried to recall what particular acts of sin and fornication we got up to at my sister's birthday party in the presence of sixteen schoolkids.

Then I remembered.

Because he looked so cute in the pink spangly fairy crown one of the little girls had shoved on top of his head, I kissed him, in the same way I had kissed the little sisters and cousins and girls at the birthday.

"I gave him a peck on the cheek!"

"What shame!" lamented my mother. "What could I tell her? 'Heh, young people, I don't know what they get up to these days'? She probably thinks that I've let you run wild! What humiliation!"

I wondered what my father would say about all this, but he was so embarrassed at the mere mention of the topic that he simply said to my mother, "That woman should control the nervous tic in her eyeballs."

In response, she turned to me and warned, "And you stop kissing that boy!"

*I*T was 10.30 p.m. I parked my car in front of the gates of his college, did the automatic head-swivel action to see if we were being watched, and then we kissed. I yanked up the gear-stick and twisted the keys to stop the motor.

He unbuckled his seat-belt and shifted about uncomfortably. "Ummm ... look what time it is."

I turned the engine back on and looked at the digital clock on the car.

"You should drive back. Your parents ... you know."

I sighed. Hand back on the brake. I knew my snatched moments of joy were selfish torments I inflicted on my parents. I knew they would be waiting up, all night if they had to, watching for my car to pull into the driveway. They would pretend they were watching television in their room, but I knew better. Sometimes, my mother's face would peer out of the window, black shadow against the flickering background.

My parents let me see as much of Michael as I wanted – twelve hours a day if I so desired – but of course there was a catch: he had to see me at our house, and I was not, under any circumstances, allowed to take him upstairs. And for that matter, if any boy could get it up in my parents' home to deflower me in the urine-stained bed I had shared with my grandmother for seven and a half years, he'd have to be extraordinarily gutsy, or have some kind of scatological obsession.

Of course, my room didn't look like the grotty history it concealed. When we moved into the new house, my parents let me keep my grandmother's bed, and for years it was the only thing in my room besides a stereo on a small black stand that had once been a Sony display cabinet at Retravision. My room was a huge, huge room for such a small, small person, and it was painted entirely in white, with heavy pink wall-to-floor curtains covering the wide windows. Smelling like Imperial Leather soap, it was exactly the sort of room one would see in an American movie, belonging to the blonde-haired sixteen-year-old sweetheart. Most of the time I didn't see what was there. I only liked the spaces. The more empty space I could make in the room, the better.

The much-loved and peed-in bed was covered in many layers, like the princess with twelve petticoats I once read about in a fairytale. It even had a faux-Victorian valance – a pale purple skirt all the way around the bottom segment, concealing four knobby wooden legs.

Once I took Michael upstairs to my room while my mother had gone out. I didn't necessarily want to sleep with him, I just wanted to see what he looked like in my room, and let the image set itself in my mind for eternity so that every time I felt the walls closing in, I would be able to pull it out of my mind like a developed Polaroid tucked carefully between the pages of an illicit diary. And then I would be able to tell myself, hah hah, I broke a rule, and the frisson and the crude sense of accomplishment in breaking the rule would be my consolation and my power.

If we really wanted to sleep with our boyfriends, as I knew many of my classmates did in high school, none of us would be stupid enough to do it at home anyway. A girl from Hong Kong in my English class lost her virginity in the cinema, but we never asked her what movie she was watching in case she burst into tears because it was inane and forgettable trash. In fact, we weren't even supposed to find out about it, except that her boyfriend thought it was a neat trick to brag to his mates, and then word got around to the girls' school and it was the end of Sherry's academic career. I saw her alone on the train, hair neatly tied back in a ponytail, staring straight ahead, pretending she couldn't see anyone. Any greetings of "Hi Sherry!" were met with suspicion – she thought that we were teasing her. Then the next time I saw her on the train it was in the lap of the boyfriend, although a few months ago she wouldn't even hold his hand in public. She sat slumped like a ventriloquist's doll and glared at any girl who dared cast looks at her boyfriend.

What did my parents think – that I was so uncontrolled I would not be able to restrain myself whenever there was a bed around? In that case, Michael and I had better not walk through the furniture department in Myer, or who knows what progeny could be created to torment us in the future, the way we were tormenting them? Or were they merely afraid that I was so stupid and meek that I would let my boyfriend take advantage of me? Probably it was the latter, because the idea of your daughter having kinky thoughts of any kind was a terrible, terrible one.

Michael entered my room awfully reluctantly because he knew we were breaking The Rule, and he was a kind boy, a decent boy, a boy who wanted to be with me not because of sex, obviously, because otherwise he could have dated the girls flinging themselves at him in college (or so I thought). He sat awkwardly on the edge of the bed, shoulders slumped, worried like hell about the return of my mother. I looked at him, and the image I saw was not one of a suave, languidly-leaning-on-one-elbow Casanova – the kind of person that my parents feared above all else. Didn't my parents know that I would not have gone for that type? Couldn't they see that Michael was more anxious than I, and that I wasn't planning to ravish him? I was nervous myself; it was the agitated frisson of pretending to do the forbidden. "I like you," I said to him. I like looking at you. I like the perfection of your eyebrows and your angular face like a Lucian Freud painting. I like your fingers that are much prettier than my own. I like the fact that you are sitting on that bed even though I told you about its distasteful history. I like the fact that you don't make a big deal out of my pretentious room. I like you sitting here and instead of being my chattel you could become a permanent fixture. I could keep you in the wardrobe and feed you bits of food, and we would be happy living this closeted existence until we were discovered.

Or more likely, until the doorbell rang.

*

"Just tell her the truth," he said to me later when my mother had left, and my shakes had started. He spoke as if the answer were that simple.

My mother had returned from picking up my sisters from school and seen me come downstairs to open the door. More importantly, she had seen Michael following behind me.

The first question she asked was, "What were you doing upstairs with the boy?"

"We were vacuuming." If my face were any straighter, you would be able to sign an affidavit above my eyebrows.

My mother said nothing, but I knew that my irrepressible desire to clean the house would be reported to my father. She left shortly afterwards without saying a word to me, to drive my sisters to their maths tutor. She didn't even yell at me, but her look said it all. It was as if I was doomed, and she was leaving me to complete whatever prurient business we were up to, because it was all too late.

And now Michael was trying to fix it up for me, feeling the burden of guilt that was with me always.

"Just tell her," he said slowly, like a benign philosophy professor with the best of intentions but so removed from the practicalities of this world that I could weep, "that you just wanted to kiss me."

I looked at him and didn't know what to say. The sheer ridiculousness of his suggestion astounded me. "I'm not even supposed to be kissing you, don't you understand? They think – or they like to think – that the most we get up to is hand-holding. So what do I tell her now, I took you upstairs because I wanted to hold your hand?"

I wasn't being fair, and I knew it. I was asking him sarcastic rhetorical questions when none of this was his fault at all. He would never understand, and not because I was a cynic and overwhelmed by the futility of it all. No, I was a realist, and I had choices to make. One of them was to keep silent about certain things, so that he would never understand, because what he did not know could not hurt him. How could I ever tell him that before my mother left us both home alone, she took me upstairs to her walk-in wardrobe and whispered, as if he could hear up a flight of stairs, a room and a wardrobe and understand Teochew dialect, "Is it safe to leave you here with him?"

"Yes," I groaned, because she was irritating me, but she had to ask me the question a couple more times, each time stressing the word "safe" with greater intensity, until my annoyance was starting to make her anxious and she thought that if she asked me anymore it might just incite me to get it on with him as an act of rebellion. She then hissed in my ear, "Don't you ever let him upstairs, you never know what he could get up to."

And he hadn't got up to anything, in fact it was me who initiated it, who invited trouble, who could not be content with innocent stolen kisses between classes but had to pose him like a doll on my purple bed, like a little girl playing with Barbie and Ken dolls.

"I'm just going to stick with my story," I said to him slowly and firmly. "We were upstairs vacuuming."

He looked at me as if I were mad. "You reckon they will believe that?"

"No, of course not."

"Then why are you telling a lie?" He couldn't understand it. "We weren't even doing anything wrong!"

"The truth, Michael," I said, "would be worse than a lie. The truth would be a threat. It would torment them forever."

"But we didn't even do anything!"

"I know."

"You're going to get into trouble."

"No kidding."

"You're shaking," he commented. Way to go, astute observer. Once the shakes started, it would be a while before they stopped. If I was only good for one thing, it was creating the first human seismograph. Michael didn't like to touch me when I was in this state, maybe he thought I was fragile, or maybe he thought that I would find it patronising. But it distressed him. The next thing he said was, "Tell her *I* told you to go upstairs."

That put a sudden end to the trembles because I was too stunned to move. I stared at him.

"No, no," he corrected himself. "Tell them that I *made* you go upstairs."

I thought the shakes had damaged my eardrums. "What?"

"Tell them I made you do it. Tell them you're not to blame. Tell them *I'm* to blame."

The consequences of my vacuuming lie were calculated to be miniscule and to protect all parties. It was nothing but a little see-through white lie, it was threat-minimisation, it was to stop the torment on both sides. But the consequences of this other lie he wanted me to tell were monstrous, earth-shattering. The consequences for him – how could he even consider *that*? Did he think I would really tell such a huge monstrous black falsehood? What on earth was he thinking? How could he take responsibility for such a thing?

"But you didn't make me do *anything*! We didn't do anything!"

He raised one eyebrow, as if to highlight that this was what he had been trying to tell me all along.

This made me think about my own stupid story about vacuuming, and to realise with devastation that I had probably instilled in him the need to lie, except that he was sincere and he did not understand the nuances of untruths, the different levels of diplomacy, the different degrees of fake. He probably thought one lie was just as good as another, and so long as you knew the truth, that was all that mattered. So why not come out with one that would get your beloved out of the most trouble? You would be unscathed because you knew the truth, and the truth would set you free. He did not understand this complicated sense of self based on others' perceptions and how one little lie about your honour could mark you down, make you a pariah or psychologically pock-mark you forever. His sense of ignorance was unwittingly brave and inadvertently defiant, and it was for this innocence that I loved him.

In the end, as I knew from the beginning, the vacuuming story worked. During dinner my father didn't say anything, because he was too embarrassed, and he could not dispute my story because to do so would be too awkward, and who knew what sordid tales could emerge. There were some things he was better off not knowing, as far as my father was concerned.

*

When I was at home, I was wearing a mask. I could not be flippant or funny or laugh too loud lest my parents thought me an uncontrollable flirt, or worse, smitten. The worst thing about our relationship was the being watched. We were putting on a show. He was trying as hard if not harder than I was to be acceptable – to be the obedient prospective son-in-law. He drank the herbal medicines my father made, and adopted what he thought was a manly reticence. He offered to help me with the dishes, and I responded automatically, "No, no, it's alright, Michael, go sit down and watch some telly."

"You know," he whispered to me one day as I was at the sink, "if we ever ... errr ... live in a domestic-type relationship, you can't do this. It unbalances things."

I didn't say anything. I didn't want to live in a domestic relationship with him, but if I did, I would have done anything to make his life easier. I owed him the world for his persistence, for his understanding. I felt guilty that he was even coming here at all. It was a one-and-a-half kilometre walk up the hill to Avondale Heights, to meet up with mediocre me, to be with me while I went about my daily duties. He was with me while I cooked and cleaned, and collected my sisters from school, and he carried my sister's purple backpack on his back.

This isn't me! I wanted to yell, *I am more exciting, there is more to me than these menial tasks, there is more to my life than what I do! I am sorry there is not much more you can see, but it's all there. You probably feel gypped.* I felt so much guilt and stress that it put my stomach in knots. My intestines had probably already macraméd a stringy bag, waiting for my heart to drop no less.

How could I compensate for wasting the youth of this unassuming boy? He was so easily made content but I still wanted to make it up to him, even though he did not expect compensation. So I washed his clothes. I made him meals. I packed his stuff when he was about to move out of college back to Perth for the summer holidays. He could have done it himself, shoved all the washed and unwashed shirts and socks into cardboard boxes, little did he care about neatly folded squares of clothes and carefully ordered cartons. It was then that I began to have my doubts, and realise the truth: that this packing, this cleaning, this fussing, was not what he appreciated about me. Anyone could have done it for him, and many girls were probably willing. Many girls were probably willing to do more.

*

But still, I drove him home every evening, and my father would want to come with us if it was getting too late – that is, past 10.30 p.m., in case I ended up twisting the car around a telephone pole. We had to weigh up the value of time – him staying longer at our house with my father accompanying us on the car-ride back to his college, or me driving him back early so that we could have the car-ride alone together. We opted for quality, not quantity.

That night, Michael looked at me with sad-labrador eyes, feeling sorry for both of us. "Now you're going to have to drive home in the dark alone. I wish you could stay over. It would be so much easier."

Easier?

He meant with him, in his bed.

His bedroom was always a mess, clothes strewn over the toughened wooden furniture that had belonged to generations of students, and socks spewing forth from every corner. Books lined his shelf – Plato, Mill, stories by Borges, drawings by Escher, and some hardcover *Sesame Street* books from childhood.

Cleaning his room, I found remnants of a life I barely knew. It lay there exposed for me, budding forth from his drawers. Photographs from an ex-girlfriend, artistically done and mounted on black cardboard – black-and-white landscapes with him in a big woollen jumper sharing the scenery with some sheep. Talk about stereotypes, I thought, you don't see me posing in photos with my homies from Footscray in a dimly lit alleyway. But in reality, I was insecure, and I was jealous because someone had looked at him from all those angles. I carefully wrapped the pictures up in a jumper, because I could tell they were precious to him, the way he looked at them wistfully. I couldn't even bring myself to look through his yearbook. There was a picture of him in there, at the college ball, with a black-haired big-bosomed girl. Another ex-girlfriend? At the very least, his date for the evening. I couldn't look at him any more. I became awkward, shy, shoulders forward, eyes downcast concentrating on what I was putting in the boxes. He had, after all, let me go through all his things. "I have nothing to hide from you," he said, and I had to honour that honesty, because I wouldn't have let him go though my stuff, never in a million years, not with my cupboard full of diaries dating from age twelve plotting Armageddon against various people who made me miserable, and a new updated will stuck at the back of every edition. I didn't want him to see all of that. This was a girl who had never travelled outside Melbourne, who lived in the same western suburbs all of her life, who spent her spare time knotting up her insides like ropes. I was a fake, and sooner or later he would find out.

I tried to tell him things. Unpleasant things, but unless I made a nice anecdote out of them it wouldn't register. I knew he liked to hear the stories about the Janome sewing machine I got for my twelfth birthday, but not the story about the pills I had to take at seventeen. As an insider, my life wasn't interesting and quirky; I was only a good storyteller, and I was running out of quirky anecdotes. I was meant to be the stoic little survivor, an everlasting fount of energy and optimism. "You know,

Alice, sometimes I wish you *would* cry," he told me, but I thought that if I did, I would be like all other girls, and I liked to think that I was different, that I was special. But in actuality I was just a better scriptwriter.

And pretty soon, I realised that the script was running out. Pretty soon he might decide to tune into new romantic comedies on other channels, and it was with this realisation that the paranoia started kicking in. I would wonder about every attractive young woman I met at parties, even when he was not there. Why me, not her? Why why why? He could probably get sex out of that one. He could get easier parents out of the other one. I knew the paranoias were mine and mine alone, demons I had to reckon with, that arose through no fault of his. Once in front of friends he made a joke about being with other girls, and I went morbidly quiet.

"Why would you get upset? Unless of course, you think it would actually happen."

He had a point there.

I found four little unopened foil packets in his room while I was packing for his journey back to Perth, and I hid them between the pages of a book I found on his shelf – *2001: A Space Odyssey*. There was no need to confront him or make a big deal out of it because of course I knew he had had sex before he met me, otherwise he might not have been so calm about waiting and waiting, and that thought didn't make me feel jealous in the way the photos did, but it did make me cautious because sooner or later being me would not be enough, and there would be no sex to keep us together, and it would be the end.

*

What would happen when I told him I didn't want to have sex? He would be understanding, and kind, but I bet he would think, *this is all your parents' doing, all these stigmas, and if you could only overcome them, you would be free*. It was either rebellion or no rebellion. We had just watched *Pleasantville* at my house after dinner, a movie about a 1950s *Brady-Bunch* world existing within a television screen, where everything was black-and-white and placidly "perfect", until some kids from half a century later enter the scene and introduce some colour into Pleasantville, and life is no longer as pleasant, but more exciting.

"I wish your parents would stop seeing in black-and-white," Michael had commented before he climbed out of the car.

But Michael, I wanted to say, it is not the matter of sex or no sex that liberates a person. I would never spend a night in your room, and you will never understand the reasons why, because you will think that it is only to do with my parents. I only get one go in this lifetime, Michael, and I don't want to screw up, literally speaking. One chance, do you understand?

But he did try to understand, to the best of his ability, because he knew the limitations, and worked carefully within them, until "We've got to be careful not to make your father aggro" became his refrain. The difficulties we faced were seen as kind of exciting, kind of heroic. Proof of our love, how much we were willing to suffer. I supposed he was suffering for the *idea* of love, but why would you suffer for someone so banal?

After a while, it probably began to dawn on him that this was not a game, that it was a series of rules and regulations, as strict as the army. He probably began to see me as a series of dos and don'ts. Once we got caught in the rain, and he said, "Oh no, what is your father going to say when he answers the

265

door and sees that I've brought you home all wet and dishevelled?" as if it was his fault that it had rained. In order to help me maintain my independence, while simultaneously appeasing my parents, he had to tread a fine line between being overly solicitous and grossly negligent. I knew it was hard on him.

We spent a lot of time in the small, dark uninhabited rooms in the attic of the Old Law Library at Melbourne University. It was our secret place, and I would block the window on the door with my shawl while we were together. I asked him whether I made him happy, which was something I had never doubted before, but now I was losing faith in my own capacities. He laughed, there was no doubt about it, he gave me his answer and I knew he meant it. He had laughed because it was a stupid question with one obvious answer, and he meant the answer.

"Do *I* make you happy?" he asked me in return, and I knew he expected the same honesty. But the only answer I could give him was a white lie, and then I started to cry. He probably thought that this confirmed what I had said, but actually I was crying because I was a liar, and the truth was that being with him made me miserable. No longer did I feel the urge to share my observations of the world with him. He could see my world for what it was – a set of rules and finely drawn lines and fraudulent erasures.

*A*ND so when his bags were all packed and he was heading back to Perth, it was the end for both of us, although he did not know it yet. He had waited for me to finish work so that he could say goodbye. I had never in my life so adored him, and my stomach had never felt so knotted.

"Where would you like to go?" I asked him, although I knew he would let me lead. That was what I loved about him. This suburb was my turf, he let me show him everything through my eyes. In the end, I decided to take him to the park where Chinese New Year was held every year. It reminded me of a few childhood days spent with my family, before the little sisters were born, when my brother and I ate barbequed corn-on-the-cob and ran away from the dragon as it approached. Our disbelief was suspended for those few moments when the dragon came to face us – we forgot that there were merely four sweating young men underneath, thrashing their limbs about to make the material move. The creature seemed to take on a life of its own. People clamoured to be near the dragon, but I shrank from its noise and violence and glaring bulging eyes.

But this was not New Year. It was dusk in summer, and the park was quiet and clean. We found a bench and sat down, facing the flowerbeds. We sat in silence for many moments. I was growing cold, and I wrapped my arms around myself. After a while, when neither of us had yet started to speak, I realised that Michael already knew. He knew that this was not a silence of ease, of familiar companionship, because he did not tell me that he was going to call me from Perth, or tell me that he was going to miss me when he left. We did not look at each other. He hummed a waiting-in-the-lift tune. He was probably trying to annoy me out of my reticence, so that we would at least have a starting basis on which to fight. *"I hate it when you hum that goddamn stupid tune!" "Well, I find it soothing and meditative." "It's crap, and you've left me with no choice but to leave. This is the end!" "You're leaving me over a tune?! No! Wait, I have more in my repertoire!"* If only it were that easy.

He sighed and picked at his fingernails. When he had produced a result that would keep a manicurist in business for the next two weeks, he put his hands away and turned to me: "You didn't bring me here so I could just say goodbye to you, did you?"

I didn't say anything.

"Because now I can't seem to say it."

I remained silent, and could not look at him.

"Because if I do, I have a feeling it is going to have more significance than just being away from each other during the summer break."

I looked at my own nails and decided I had some wrecking work to do.

"I'm right, aren't I?"

I remained silent.

"Oh. I see. You brought me here to tell me something."

I finally looked at him.

"Then tell me."

So I did.

It started with the three words that I was taught always to keep to myself, to expect from men, but never, ever to give away. The three words that caused my grandmother to fight all her life, the very three words that compelled my mother to leave her family and walk through three countries by foot to spend the rest of her life in an alien land that she would never understand, and that would never understand her.

And the consequences of the three words to me, for me, how real they were.

When I had finished, he didn't look at me for a long while. He looked at his hands, fingers curled towards the palm. Then he finally looked at me with ... what? Disappointment? Hurt? Perhaps even contempt, which I had never seen before. But one thing I did not see in his gaze, as hard as I looked, was surprise. For that I was relieved.

"You think," he told me, "that love is this 'one true love for ever and ever' kind of thing, don't you?"

That was probably contempt I saw on his face.

"No, that's not true."

But perhaps it was.

Yet how could I explain how sometimes having the right feelings was just not enough, how it was never enough, for a "forever kind of thing" – a decision you make for life, for better and for worse, and how I did not want to make this decision at eighteen.

"But you don't have to. Geez, it's not like we are going to get married anytime soon or anything!"

Yet I knew that the dating was over, the honey in the honey-moon period was way past its expiry date. He would find other girls to adore him. If this went any further, I would be doomed because I would doom myself. Secondhand goods. I adored him. It was so easy to make him happy, I just had to be me. But time was running out, *I* was running out, there wasn't much left of me to give. I didn't want to give him faulty goods because he was the type of boy who would never ask for a refund. And the only thing of value left of me to give him would leave me valueless. Dented washing machine no one wants to use.

"I wrote you a poem," he told me, "I was going to give it to you."

I said nothing.

He looked at me. "Would you still have done this if I had given it to you?"

I looked back at him. He thought that a poem could change the course of things. It reminded me of that young mother in the fifth deck of the *Titanic*, who read her two little children fairytales as the ship was sinking.

"Yes. I would have still done this, Michael."

I seemed to care bugger-all for lofty romance.

I seemed to care bugger-all for feelings. "I'm sorry."

He began to cry. I had not expected this. I didn't know what to do. I wiped his nose with my sleeve because there were no tissues around. This seemed to make him even more upset, so I had to use the other sleeve.

"Come on, it's snot that bad."

He stopped sniffing. He stared at me.

"My God, it's terrible!"

"No …"

"Bloody awful!"

"No, come on …"

"Hell, that was atrocious! Never heard such a bad joke. You should be *pun*-ished for it!"

"Damn you! What about yours?" I retorted, and somehow those words had a tear-triggering effect because pretty soon I was in dire need of tissues or at least uncharted terrain on my sleeves. "Damn you, Michael!"

"This is worse than the time we ate raw chilli at that restaurant to see who was more stoic." Of course we both remembered. Fanciest place in Footscray, with butcher's paper on the tables on top of the white tablecloths, and there we were, not realising that our dates were numbered.

We sat in silence, and the sun set. It grew colder, and we wrapped our arms around ourselves, tacitly knowing that we were now already separate, that we could no longer allow ourselves to keep each other warm.

Finally, he looked at me. "Well, I'm going to miss you."

"I'm going to miss you, too."

We sat like that for a long time, not speaking, knowing this was the last time we would be sitting together like this. We were just-ended lovers in a sense. Lovers in the sense that we loved each other wholeheartedly, with a sort of childhood faith.

"We'd better be heading off."

We did not look at each other as we walked down to the station.

"I still don't understand, Alice," he finally said as we reached our destination.

But he did not doubt that I loved him, because I had wiped his nose with my sleeve. I waited for the train with him, and it soon arrived.

"Well, goodbye then."

"Goodbye, Michael."

And there I was, a solitary girl in a sales uniform, standing on Platform 1 of Footscray station watching the 8.43 p.m. Flinders Street train leave and snake its way past the graffiti-covered concrete walls and into the grassy wilderness of no-man's industrial wasteland. If this were a film, it would be about now that there would be a shot of a single extended arm out the window of the train, and then the close-up of the hero's tear-stained face would fade away and the credits would start to roll, perhaps accompanied by some poignant, bittersweet tune.

I knew that Michael would go home and unpack his carefully packed suitcases. He would find the little presents I had left him – photographs, books, toiletries, cards. He might even smile upon discovering what I had carefully packed between the pages of his copy of *2001: A Space Odyssey*. "Crazier than I thought," he would think, and take out the four or so foil packages and throw them in the bin, because it's not like he couldn't buy them again. And in time, I hoped, he would think of me with a certain fondness, despite the girlfriends to come and the ones that had gone before.

And I would go home and continue the other play, the one that has not ended, the one that will never end, and I would resume my role as "dutiful daughter", this time with more understanding and compassion.

I could see my mother at my same age, riding on the back of my father's bicycle in Vietnam, her hands around his waist, the excitement and frisson of trying to evade the bicycle behind her – her sister Ly was always tagging along. I could see her trying as I did, as hard as I did, to get some time alone with the man she loved, to forget about the drudgeries of work and duty and let her hair fly loose and revel in her youth and beauty, and the fact that this man nine years her senior, her former boss for crying out loud, thought that she was the most incredible, delightful, charming creature to have graced the earth. So much so that he was willing to take her to a foreign country of which the only thing he knew was that it didn't snow, and to live with her for the rest of his life and see their lives multiply into four new ones.

*

My parents were sitting at the dining table when I arrived home. I pretended that the pollen count was really high out there, on this wattle-scented summer night, and that my eyes were red because of that.

"Good to see you home not so late tonight," commented my father. I rubbed at my eyes and moaned a little more about the curse of hay-fever as I slumped on our green leather living-room sofa.

From the couch, I watched my parents out of the corner of my eye. My mother was wearing her pink terry-towelling bath-robe over her green jumper, white tracksuit pants and brown knitted vest. On her head was her red, white and blue Western Bulldogs beanie with the pom-pom on the top. She didn't barrack for any football team, she had found the beanie on special at Forges for ninety-nine cents. My father was wearing his flannelette pyjamas with his old brown leather jacket over the top, the same one he wore to work every morning instead of a suit jacket. I watched my mother cut up a mango, with one of our two kitchen knives. She handed half of it to my father.

273

He took it and I watched them both sharing a mango, the messiest of fruit, with no sense of delicacy whatsoever. It had taken over twenty years of marriage to achieve this familiarity, the same kind of unselfconsciousness of children sharing a snack, the complete ease and abandonment of self.

I watched my parents for a little while longer, and then headed upstairs to bed. I knew that tomorrow I would have to tell them about tonight, but it could wait until the morning. Let them eat their mango in peace.

Epilogue

"What are you doing, Alice?"

My sister Alina's face peered down at me, with her eyelashes that pointed down towards her cheeks, just like my grandmother's.

"I'm looking at the sky." The sky was as clear and blue as a child's new crayon, as it had been the first time we visited this park, the second time, and every other time.

"Why?"

"Because."

"Lying on the grass is going to make you itchy, Alice."

"Doesn't matter."

"What are you looking at?"

"Just the sky."

"I'm gonna look too."

"Okay. Lie down on your back."

"Okay."

A few moments later: "Hey Alice, what am I supposed to be looking at?"

"Up."

"But what?"

"Just up." I thought she should discover the pictures in the clouds herself.

Soon, three other little cousins trotted over and wanted to lie on their backs too. They blinked at the sky for a while.

"I'm bored."

"There are no good clouds."

"Why are we doing this?"

"'Cause Alice is."

The clouds moved, and I imagined a mirror in the sky, reflecting the world back in reaffirming white whorls.

"Ay!"

I heard a piercing yell from behind me.

"Agheare, what the hell do you think you're doing?" My mother.

I turned my head to one side, towards the direction of the sound.

"My holy sacred Buddha, look at her, nineteen and lying flat on her back on the grass like that! With no shame. And look what's happening, now all the little ones are following her!"

I looked back up at the sky. I could hear her telling my father what I had been doing. I knew he would just look at us and laugh. I turned my head towards the party assembled in front of the only pink and orange grave among the black granite ones in Lilydale Memorial Park.

Aunt Que set down her vat of mixed bean soup on top of the grave. Aunt Samso set down her fried noodles. Aunt Anna set down her Continental pasta bake. And Aunt Jasmine set down her huge pot of chicken curry, grinning at Uncle Frank because even though they were well into their sixties, they were still in love.

The rest of the food was laid out on the polished pink and orange marble – as fine as any marble you would find on any table at any one of our mock-Georgian houses. "Eight thousand dollars," grinned Uncle Frank, knocking his knuckles on the shiny surface. "I helped pick it out. Beautiful hah?" Aunt Jasmine beamed up at him.

I sat up as Aunt Anna handed me five bunches of plastic flowers to arrange. Shoving the stems of fake flora into a real china vase, I tried in vain to match the opal blue poppies with the magenta gerberas. No flowers were ever that blue in real life, nor did they have black plastic stamens that stuck out like big-headed nails. Since trying to achieve realism with these specimens was as likely as painting a Renoir with half a dozen textas, I opted for a striking Ikea-catalogue effect instead.

"Wah!" cried Aunt Que, "what a miserly effort! They're all going to blow away with the wind!" And before I knew it, she had shoved in at least three more bouquets, including a dozen neon-green and white roses with glue-dew-drops. She plugged in every possible breathing space at the neck of the vase, and it choked out a few leaves before becoming completely still. The breath of afternoon breeze couldn't even stir a petal, they were jammed so close. "Now it's much better. Look at all the colours!"

I looked. The flower arrangement was at least five times larger than the vase itself.

"That's enough with the flowers. Now let's light the incense," said Uncle Frank.

We all lined up to collect our stick of incense, and to bow

down in front of the HUYEN THAI embossed into the granite in gold letters.

"Buddha bless our mother," mumbled my parents, aunties and uncles.

"Buddha bless our grandmother," mumbled my siblings, cousins and I.

The incense was slowly burning down, swirls of smoke drifting up like silk kite tails towards the sky. I sat on the grass and watched. In the centre of the tombstone was our surname PUNG written in gold with the sweeping strokes of Chinese calligraphy. On the right-hand side was my grandmother's picture with the dates 1911–2002 underneath, and on the left was my grandfather's picture – 1907–1975. The rest of the Chinese I could not read.

"Is Grandpa also buried in there?" asked Alison, peering at the headstone.

"No."

"Then why is his picture there?"

"So that we remember him."

I knew that the grave was housing a mere empty shell, that my *real* grandmother had left before her burial. Probably off to find my grandfather and resume that argument they were having a quarter-century ago before Pol Pot separated them.

"It's so deep!" my sister Alison had exclaimed when she tossed her handful of rice and grains into the open grave at my grandmother's burial three years before. "I can't even see the bottom." I wondered now whether things were growing with the grains we tossed in, like the life that grew above my great-grandmother, all that rice and abundance on top of the killing fields. All that growth that grew all that produce that created all that life that made all that food on top of my grandmother's grave. The food in steaming pots. Two little bowls of rice and two little bowls of tea arranged on either side of the incense pot with perfect symmetry – even when the souls have sighed out of their bodies, you still must accord your parents equal respect. Suddenly, my eyes caught something unexpected, something quirkily out of place amid all the plastic tofu-containers and steam-breathing mounds of food. Behind all the pots and plates, the grapes and geraniums, there were four shining gold Easter bunnies. Where had they come from?

"My sister bought them," Cousin Tammy told me, "for the little ones."

I remembered how, at my grandmother's burial, before the earth was levelled on top of her plot, lucky red candies had been handed out to everybody, the same ones that Little Brother had yearned for all that time ago. Some things never change. We had unwrapped our brown and pink caramels and watched the bulldozers slowly come in. When we walked away from the grave, we were told that under no circumstances were we to turn and look back. We were to keep walking forward, sucking on our lollies.

We still believed in silly superstitions and sweet endings after all.

*

When I was seven, Granny was living with us, in our old house, along with kind Uncle Wilson, Auntie Anna and cousins Andrew and Angela fresh from the Fragrant Harbour. They had a partitioned portion of our living room separated by a curtain my father made out of bedsheets. One day Granny came back from Coles supermarket with a white plastic bag, and from her wrinkled hands emerged wonders never before seen by my seven-year-old eyes. Four little solid eggs, two medium-sized eggs and one small Easter bunny for each of us. "Don't eat them all at once," she told us.

My four-year-old brother set to work at once, unwrapping his first little egg. I set to work with my paper and stapler, making a box in which to put my little polished gems. Cousin Andrew lasted two days, and then he couldn't help himself.

"They're empty!" he cried, after he bit off a part of his bunny's ear and could see through the hole.

"Yeah? So?"

"Back in Hong Kong bunnies are filled. All of it's chocolate." He felt gypped but I didn't care, I expected the hollowness. While everyone else's sources of joy were rapidly depleting, the remnants adhering to their sticky faces, I still had my six eggs and a bunny. They were hand-boxed, wrapped in a grey plastic bag and hidden in my bottom drawer where no prying family members could ever find them.

I wanted mine to last as long as I could, I wanted a collection. After four days, I did not even think about eating them. The besetting temptation was no longer there, or if it was, I muffled it. *Eat me! Eat me!* the Bunny pleaded with its crayon-blue eyes and Red Tulip lips. I glared at it. *Be quiet.* Then I wiped away its tears – for an edge of the foil had mysteriously ripped – with my sleeve, and put it back in the box, back in the bag, back in the bottom of the drawer.

Every day, my brother and cousin would ask whether I had eaten any, and every day I would smile and give them the same reply. After two weeks, they stopped asking. After three weeks, I stopped the daily check on my hoard, my nest eggs. I knew they were still there. I knew I had self-control, and I knew soon I would be the richest girl in the whole of Bliss St, Braybrook. Dedication, preservation, reward – I had it down pat.

Then, four weeks later, I decided that one of the little ones had to go. It was time. I imagined they were quivering in their cotton-wool padded prison, I was so excited. But when the drawer was opened – horror of all horrors, worse than finding my fortunes furtively stolen – ants spilled out and the bunny had melted and the goo that gushed from the eggs had wrecked my box. I didn't care about the ants that would crawl up my arms, I pulled the whole drawer out of the cupboard and dug my hands in deep. While Alexander and Andrew watched, I started pulling out each egg one by one – or what was left of them – trying in desperation to find one that was not insect-infested, trying to sort through the foil and frustration, not wanting to believe that these squished tragedies were once my pride and joy, the things I had looked forward to most in the world for more than four weeks.

"Don't cry," said my grandmother, kneeling down to have a look herself. "I will buy you new ones, don't cry." But I wasn't even going to cry, crying was the last thing on my mind. I was beyond tears, I could not believe that one little tear in a bunny's ear could lead to this devastation.

"Don't cry," said my mother, as she took the drawer to the sink. "That's what you get for keeping things for too long, you see. Look at the mess I have to clean out now!"

"What are you doing?" my grandmother admonished me, as she opened up my fingers one by one and removed the melted mess from my hand. "It's no good now, you can't save it. Listen to me, we'll buy you new ones."

"But I don't want new ones," I replied firmly.

"Don't be silly."

"Don't be difficult."

But I wasn't being difficult. I wiped my hands on my green pants handed down from Cousin Andrew. New ones would just not be the same. I would never go to the same trouble again. "It doesn't matter anyway."

My mother and my grandmother did not say anything, but my grandmother came to help my mother dig the remnants of the gift from the bottom of the drawer, and they did not yell at me for making such a mess of things.